REFORMIST AND CONSERVATIVE TEACHERS

REFORMIST AND CONSERVATIVE TEACHERS

A Sociological Study

By

AZRA ABIDI

ANMOL PUBLICATIONS PVT. LTD.
NEW DELHI - 110 002 (INDIA)

ANMOL PUBLICATIONS PVT. LTD.
4374/4B, Ansari Road, Daryaganj
New Delhi - 110 002
Ph.: 3261597, 3278000
Visit us at: www.anmolbooks.com

Reformist and and Conservative Teachers

First Edition, 2003

ISBN 81-261-1415-0

PRINTED IN INDIA

Published by J.L. Kumar for Anmol Publications Pvt. Ltd., New Delhi - 110 002 and Printed at Tarun Offset Printers.

Dedicated

to

My Parents

Contents

Foreword

The strength of a nation is largely dependent upon the kind and amount of education of its people. The great Sufi Saint Kabir says the teacher is like a potter and the pupil is like clay. It is the teacher who shapes and moulds the personality of the pupil. In India the status of a teacher has always remained very high. Called as "guru" in yore days he has been commanding deep respect and veneration not only of the pupils but also of parents and the entire society. Thus responsibility for shaping the destiny of the nation rests on the teachers. As such the teaching is more than a profession is a mission.

It is not necessary that one may adopt any change in the social area of life, may greet every change with ease in another areas of life like personal and religious. So who accepts the changes in all areas of life with joy and comfort, may be called a radical person. Etymologically a radical is one who is concerned with on tending to concentrate on fundamental aspect of a matter, searching or thoroughgoing and favours change and reforms. A radical, is a daring person whose flexibility stand him in good stead in welcoming and negotiating social change. As a general rule a radical is far more flexible than conservative one. A conservative is rather a security minded and continuous person who likes to play safe. He feels at home with the traditional ways of life which involve hardly any social risk, nor make a call on his ingenuity of his traditional self walked up against the sea of social changes around.

Applying radicalism vs. conservatism to teachers it is

desirable that teacher must be radical at a time, despite being conservative to some extent as to recognise healthy traditional customs and social values is also equally significant. In a highly changing multiracial, multilingual and multiethnic society like ours to be radical is virtuous.

A conservative teacher always plays with the teaching profession and student's mind. Since every student and every institution is equally significant. University and college teachers produce two kinds of impact with their teaching acts. First, proper working of the teaching is assured and secondly their own teaching skill is tested. The focus of the present work by Dr. Azra Abidi is on sociological study of university and college level teacher's attitude towards conservatism and radicalism in three areas of their life — personal, social and religious. The findings of this work shows that female teachers are more radical in comparison of male teachers. Instead of few teachers, most of the teachers were radical in their personal, social and religious areas of life. Dr. Azra Abidi noted that few teachers were in the category of highly conservative that means they influenced hundreds of students and the result would be that hundreds of conservatives would be there to hinder the progress of nation. It is necessary for the democratic secular India that there should be more and more radical teachers in our colleges and universities.

In agreement with the findings of Dr. Azra Abidi's present research venture, I am confident this book will prove informative and useful to teaching community and the researchers in the field of sociology.

—Professor Mohini Anjum
Dept. of Sociology
Jamia Millia Islamia

New Delhi

Acknowledgements

This book is substantially based on the findings of my doctoral research carried out at the University of Lucknow.

The role of the Teacher in our modernizing Indian Society is multifaceted. He is called upon to take up enormous responsibilities, bear the miseries, pains on defections inherent in the job situation and make many sacrifices, both personal and professional. The problem of this marginality in teachers behaviour requires a scientific explanation.

In this work it has been endeavoured to present an overall review of such measures. The subject wide and varied as it is can not possibly be dealt a length in one of these alone.

I cherish the encouragement and motivation that I received from my mentor Dr. Rashid Ali Syed (Professor, Dept. of Sociology, Lucknow University), who not only provided me all the wherewithal, but was gracious enough to spare sufficient time towards completion of this study.

I shall be failing in my duty, if I do not mention the whole hearted co-operation that Mr. S.G.S. Kazmi, my husband extended to me in making available the requisite literature and preparing index for the book.

I received excellent cooperation and generous help at all levels, both from teaching officials of the Department of Sociology, Jamia Millia Islamia, New Delhi, where at present I am working and from my family side too.

I record my special thanks to all my friends and to my publisher M/s. Anmol Publications Pvt. Ltd., New Delhi, who not only understood the academic/research idiom and medium in proper perspective, but also took extra care to give present shape to this publication.

— Dr. Azra Abidi

Chapter 1
Introduction

Change is a universal phenomenon and no society can exist without change. Hence it is said change is an essential feature of society. Man's life itself is a good example of change. From his birth to old age, the man passes through many stages of change. Our society has reached to the present age of civilization from the prehistoric savage age through such changes. Had there been no change in our society, we would have still remained in the same savage age of the history. Together with the change in different ages, there were also changes in the wants and needs of the human beings. First these wants were less and limited, but with the advancement of the society human wants multiplied considerably and gave impetus to a system of imparting education to the people. School and colleges were considered as the best institution of imparting education to the children. So with the growth of schools and colleges, the concept of formal education came in to existence. Teachers are indispensable element of school. A school and college can be run without a building and adequate resources, but seldom a school and college can be run without teachers.

"The strength of a nation" writes Moffitt, *"is largely dependent upon the kind and amount of education of its people"*.[1] Education in any country reflects the needs and aspirations of its people. These needs and aspirations are never static because the new

environmental forces bring about constant change in the life, and ideals of society. The increasing complexity of modern life brings growing insistence on more and more effective education. In India, new economic and social pressmen are making more and more exacting demands on education. The teachers initial education and preparation and continuous efforts determine the quality of education and ultimately the strength and quality of education. Education is considered a principal factor of change. Through education we can remove any evil of the society. In removing these evils teachers play a pivotal role and hence they are called *"agents of social change"*. The attitudes and personality of teachers greatly influence the students. So it is essential that the teacher should have open mind and radical at times.

Teaching has a pivotal place in a civilized society. Right from the beginning of civilization teaching profession has been regarded as the noblest profession. It has to fulfill the ultimate aim of creating a sober and a healthy society by laying a firm foundation of character building, social efficiency, spread of nationalism and happiness. In ancient India the status of a teacher always remained very high. He has been called the "Guru" commanding deep respect and veneration not only of the pupils but also of parents and the entire society. Thus, the profession of teaching has been considered a mission.

"Teaching" as Mr. Joad[2] says, "is not everybody's cup of tea". The teacher is a source of dynamic force for all the school activities. Building and equipment are important. So one curricula and books, but in absence of a genuine teacher all these things become meaningless. The teacher occupies a very important place in the school system. Apart from imparting knowledge to the pupil, he influences them in difficult ways.

Habits, attitudes, beliefs and values that a child develops are to a large extent influenced by the teacher. He has a powerful and abiding influence in the formation of the character of every future citizen. The teacher acts as a pivot for the transmission of intellectual, technical skills and cultural tradition from one generation to the other.

According to Gibran[3] "The teacher who walks in the shadow of the temple among his followers, gives not only of his wisdom but rather of his faith and his lovingness".

In the words of Shamuddin,[4] "The plant of freedom which has been planted with the help of martyrs should now be grown and made to bloom like a lovely flower by the teachers as building of new nation".

The role of a teacher in a society is well known to all. The nation's well being depends on the care for teachers. Kothari Commission has very aptly observed that the future of the nation is shaped in its class rooms. A teacher has been given a key position in the educational process of the country. He is said to be a nation builder, a guide, a torch bearer and transmitter of knowledge to crown it all. He plays a vital role in shaping the nation's destiny. He is a powerful instrument for social regeneration and reconstruction of the country.

Teacher occupies front place in the educational machinery. The main actor on the educational stage is the teacher of all the participants in the drama of education. The role of the teacher is significant and full of responsibility.

It is the teacher that moulds the most precious human resources of the land viz., the young students in their impressionable age to their full bloom.

Prof. K.G. Saiyedain[5] role of the teacher quite illustrative when he says that, "The teacher has to patiently cutout of a crude and unshaped stone in to a thing of beauty proportion and balance".

The teacher who is the architect of the new generation has to mould the mind and chisel the attitude of the young. Education is a comprehensive and synthetic process which aims at harmonious development of the body, mind, emotion and spirit of the talent of students. While the fundamental aim of education is the same at all times. The emphasis has to shift from one aspect to another period to suit the varying ethos.

A true teacher instead of feeling of bored by daily routine will rather equip himself by constant practice. A teacher in the true sense of the term is a transforming personality. Rightly it has been remarked that the teacher is not an instructor or a task master but a helper and a guide. His business is to guide and not to impose. He does bring perfection of the pupil's mind, he only shows him how to perfect his instruments of knowledge and keeps and encourages him in the process. University and college level teachers are more important than the other teachers because their students are generally more attached to them emotionally as well as psychologically also.

The attitude of the students of university and college level are influenced by many factors and the personality of teacher and their attitude is one of the important factor. This is the reason that university and college level teachers should be open minded, progressive and radical so that the students should be positively influenced towards radicalism.

University and degree level teachers should not only teach their subjects properly to the students but also introduce progressive ideas to them. They should also help students to satisfy their psychological and intellectual needs.

The teacher's behaviour influences the behaviour of the student, hence a conservative teacher would influence hundreds of students and the result would be that hundreds of conservatives would be there to hinder the progress of the nation, whereas a radical teacher would influence hundreds of students towards progressive ideas and radicalism. Hence it is more important that radical teacher should be more but it is sad that in our country there are very few radical teachers in our colleges and universities.

The future present in the ancient system of education are unfortunately conspicuous by their absence in the present days. We no longer find the ancient glory of the teacher. The situation reflects the teacher's present status. The pupil-teacher relationship at present is quite different from what prevailed in those days. Prof. S.N. Mukherji remarks that *"the present day teacher has no status, no stability of service and consequently no peace of mind"*. All the attributes paid to the profession like nation building, *"man making"*, *"noble"* and *"sacred"* are only high sounding empty words.

People differ in their behaviour towards radicalism and conservatism, one person may greet every change with joy, considering it a step towards a better society. There are other type of people who dread changes. They look back to the good old days. These differences in attitude and behaviour tend to fall somewhere along a conservative-radical continuum, somewhere between opposing and favouring social change.

The concept of radicalism-conservatism usually have been associated with the area of politics, that is having political meanings. In this sense of the terms conservatism-radicalism may be used to divide the vast array of political ideologies into two gross categories of right and left. In this study the conservative and radical terms are used to cover the behaviour of university and college teachers in various areas of the life namely bio-data, family background, political background, Activism, organizational setup etc.

The social philosophy which tends to resist change, and to adhere to and support the established order the basic source of social stability. It has been long recognized that there is a sort of philosophical antagonistic cooperation between stability and progress, permanence and change. Conservatism represents the valuation of the old, the tried, the familiar, the dependable. As ordinarily used, the term *"conservatism"* frequently carries an implication of development to the degree it becomes an obstacle to social progress.

Who is conservative? Who has attitude of conservatism? Conservative is a person who clings to the status quo. Opposing all changes on the assumption that anything new is going to be worse. He reveres his past and in the one believing that *"nothing should be tried for the first time, who learns nothing and forgets not"*. (Fairchild Dictionary of Sociology)

In the words of Burke (1951), *"... a conservative outlook is that man's traditional inheritance in rich, grand endlessly proliferated and mysterious, deserving of veneration and not to be cast away lightly in favour of the narrow uniformity, unless it is necessary to change, it is necessary not to change"*. (Hearmshaw, 1933)

Reginald Northman writes, "We *may write the world conservative with a big "C" or a small one either as representing the principles of the conservatism party or a well known attitude of the human mind, without doubt conservatism with a small "c" has its influence on political conservatism whereas the emphasis of the latter however, merely on an aversion to change and a distrust of what has not been tested by experience and nothing else than it would be barren indeed"*. Conservatives always stressed the necessity for preserving the spirit of religion and its organization, and this is affectation because their faith is deeply rooted in the foil out of which our tradition has grown and inherent in it are certain religious beliefs and certain conceptions of man's listing. *A greater sense of religion would assist in the solution of many of our problems.*(Reginald Northman, *Conservatism the Only Way*)

A conservative is rather a security-minded and cautious person, who likes to play safe. He feels at home with the traditional ways of life which involve hardly and social risk, nor make a call on his ingenuity of his traditional self walked up against the sea of social changes around. *"Radicalism generally has been held to be the advocacy of ideas and beliefs at variance with those of the majority of the group, community or society"*. (Lemert, 1951)

To be sure, radicalism is a conspicuous departure from deeply established social habits which have the stamp of social approval. More scientifically of course radicalism designates social ideas which support to go to the root of things and work therefrom for drastic and sweeping changes in the existing institutions. In terms of the processes of social change, the frame of mind called radicalism is a style which develops as a reaction to the diehard orthodoxy's of the past and the present.

A radical on the other hand is a daring person whose flexibility stands him in good stead in welcoming and negotiating social change with ease. As general rule a radical person is far more flexible than a conservative one. But a case can be made out to show that extreme radicalism is capable of degenerating into a sort of conservatism and dogmatism when for example, a radical is sold on a particular ideology and is so deeply conditioned by it that he virtually becomes a prisoner of it, his mind gets closed and he refuses stubbornly to see another point of view, however rational or relevant.

TRADITIONALISM AND CONSERVATISM

Is conservatism a phenomenon universal to all mankind, or is it an entirely new product of the historical and sociological conditions of our own times? The answer is that both sorts of conservatism exist. On the one hand there is the sort that is more or less universal and on the other hand, there is the definitely modern sort which is the product of particular historical and social circumstances and which has its own peculiar traditions, forms and structure. We could call the first type "*natural conservatism*"[6] and the second one "*modern conservatism*" where it is not that the word '*natural*' is already heavily burdened with many different meanings. It will perhaps be better therefore if we adopt Max Weber's term '*traditionalism*' to denote the first type so that when we speak of '*conservatism*' we shall always mean '*modern*' conservatism — '*something essentially different from mere traditionalism*'.

Traditionalism signifies a tendency to cling to vegetative patterns to old ways of life which we may well consider as fairly ubiquitous and universal. Traditionalism is not therefore necessarily bound up, even today with political or other sorts of conservatism. *'Progressive'* people for instance regardless of their political convictions may often act *'traditionalistically'* to a very large extent in many other spheres of lives.

The word *'traditionalist'* describes what, to a greater or less degree is a formal psychological characteristics of every individuals mind. *'Conservative'* action however, is always dependent on a concrete set of circumstances. There is no means of knowing in advance what form a *'conservative'* action in the political sense will take, whereas the general attitude implied in the term *'traditionalist'* action will be like. This much is clear however, that acting along conservative lines involves more than automatic responses of a certain type, it means that the individual is consciously or unconsciously guided by a way of thinking and acting which has its own history behind it, before it comes into contact with the individual.

Conservatism (political) is therefore an objective mental structure as opposed to the, 'subjectivity' of the isolated individual. In one word conservative is not an objective entity in any rightly or wrongly understood Platonist sense of the preexistence of ideas. But as compared with the experience of the particular individual it has the certain very definite objectivity.

Conservatism is just such and historically developed, dynamic, objective structural configuration. People experience and act in 'conservative' way is so far, and only in so far as they incorporate themselves into one of the phase of the development of this objective mental structure either simply reproducing it in whole or in part, or by developing it further by adopting it to a particular concrete situation.

Only when the peculiar nature of the objectivity of a dynamic structural configuration has been grasped can one be in a position to distinguish 'conservative' from 'traditionalism ' behaviour.

Traditionalist behaviour is almost purely reactive[7] conservative behaviour is meaningful and moreover is meaningful in relation to circumstances which change from epoch to epoch. It is therefore clear why their is no necessary contradiction in the fact that, a politically progressive man can react in an entirely traditionalist way in his everyday life. In the political sphere he lets himself be guided more or less.

Consciously, by an objective, structural configuration, in his everyday life his behaviour is merely reactive. Two points now arise. Firstly, the term 'conservatism' must not be assumed to be purely a political one although on the whole, as we shall see its political aspect is perhaps rather more important one. Conservatism also implies a general philosophical and emotional complex which may even constitute a definite style of thought. Secondly, conservatism as an objective historical structural configuration must not be assumed to include no traditionalist elements within itself quite the contrary, we shall see in fact that conservatism takes a particular historical form of traditionalism and develops it to its logical conclusions.

Nevertheless, in spite of this apparent overlapping of the two phenomena or may be even because of it, the distinction between merely traditionalist and conservative behaviour is a very clear one. Precisely because of its purely formal semi-reactive nature, traditionalist behaviour has practically no traceable history whereas conservatism, on the other hand, is an entity with a clear historical and social continuity. Which has arisen and developed in a particular historical and social situation, as the best of all guides to history-language-clearly demonstrates; the very word 'conservatism' is a new one of comparatively recent origin.

It was Chateaubri who first lent the word its peculiar meaning when he called the periodical he issued to propagate the idea of the clerical and political restoration, the conservative.[8] The word entered into general use in Germany in the thirties[9] and was officially adopted in England in 1835.[10] We can take the emergence of a new terminology to indicate the emergence of a new social phenomenon, although of course it tells us little about the latter's actual nature.

The Sociological Background of Modern Conservatism

Modern conservatism differs from traditionalism primarily in that it is a function one particular historical and situation. Traditionalism is general psychological attitude which express itself in different individuals as a tendency to cling to the past and a fear of innovation. But this elementary psychological tendency may attain a special function in relation to social process. What was formerly miserly a psychological character is lies common to all men, under certain circumstances becomes central factor lending coherence to a particular trend in the social process.

This development of the traditionalist attitude into the nucleus of a definite social trend does not take place spontaneously; it takes place as a response to the fact that 'progressivism' had already constituted itself as a definite trend.

Traditionalism is essentially one of those dormant tendencies which each individual unconsciously harbors within himself. Conservatism, on the other hand is conscious and reflective from the first, since it arises as a counter-movement in conscious opposition to the highly organized, coherent and systematic 'progressive' movement.

The emergence of a conscious conservative movement is therefore already an indication that the modern social and intellectual world has developed a particular structure of its own. The mere existence of conservatism as a coherent trend means that history developing more and more in terms of the interaction of such comprehensive 'trends' and 'movements', some of which are 'progressive' and further social change, while others are 'retrogressive' and retard it.

That such 'trends' can arise is explained by the fact that society today is gradually achieving a new dynamic unity, at the expense of all the old scattered self. Contained provincial feudal units which are increasingly absorbed into national units; these latter may later coalesce further into supranational ones. Although at first nations remain to a large extent socially and culturally autonomous, the fundamental economic and social problem in all modern states is so structurally similar that it is not surprising that parallel social and intellectual divisions are reproduced in them all.

These structural problems common to all modern states include the following:

(i) The achievement of national unity.

(ii) The participation of the people in the government of the country.

(iii) Incorporation of the state in the world economic order.

(iv) Solution of the social questions.[11]

They appear to be of such importance for the social as well as for the intellectual life of the community that there is a marked tendency for all divisions within it to develop in close relation to the tensions arising from attempts to solve these fundamental problems of social structure. Religious struggle have gradually been transformed into political struggles and in the English revolution political divisions can already been clearly seen through the guise of religious divisions. The nearer we approach the nineteenth century, the more does this becomes true of other intellectual phenomena as well and the more easily can they be described along party lines in terms of their direct or indirect relation to social and political problems.

Accordingly, at the same time as a conscious functionalized, political conservatism emerges as a distinct political force imply also a particular form of experience and thought. At approximately the same times as, or perhaps even a little earlier than, political conservatism, these emerged a corresponding Weltanschauung and conservative mode of thought. 'Conservative' and 'liberal' in our terminology in relation to the first half of the nineteenth century signify something more than different political aims. The terms imply in each case a quite specific affinity with quite different philosophies and therefore also imply quite different moods of thought. Thus the word 'conservative' connects, so to speak, an entire comprehensive world structure; the sociological definition of this word (which necessarily includes more than its historical political definition) must therefore take into account that historical, configuration which brought forth a new term as the expression of a new fact.

To find out why 'modern conservatism' emerged so late in history, we must turn to the various historical and social factors the conjunction of which provided the prerequisite conditions for its development. The following factors occurring together would appear to create the necessary historical and sociological conditions for the rise of conservatism.

(i) The status of historical-social forces must cease to be a static one. It must become a dynamic process of oriented change. Individual events must to an increasing extent in every sphere point to the key problem of the growth of the social body. At first conscious and voluntary, and at the same time the exact importance of each element for the development of the whole will become clearer. The number of isolated self-sufficient social units which previously existed will also diminish accordingly. The most common place action, however unimportant in itself, will now contribute something to the general processes of development and either further on hinder it[12], and it becomes increasingly possible to describe every event and very attitude in terms of its function in relation to the development of society as a whole.

(ii) Further the dynamics of this process must to an increasing extent desire from social differentiation. Different classes must arise horizontal social groupings, reacting to events in a more or less homogeneous way. Some will tend to push social development forward, while others will hold it up, or even consciously work to set it back.

(iii) Further, ideas must also be differentiated along these lines, and the major trends in thought, whatever mixtures and syntheses may be produced, must correspond to the broad lines of this social differentiation.

(iv) Finally, this social differentiation (into groups with different functions in relation to the social process—some forwarding and others retarding it) must take on increasingly (and later even a purely economic) character.[13]

The political factor must be autonomous, and must become the primary nucleus around which new grouping crystallize.

To put it briefly, the development and widespread existence of conservatism, as distinct from traditionalism, is due in the last report to the dynamic character of the modern world; to the basis of this dynamic in social differentiation to the fact that this social differentiation tends to draw the human intellect along with it and forces it to develop along its own lines; and finally to the fact that the basic aims of the different social groups do not merely crystallize ideas into actual movements of thought, but also create different antagonistic Weltanschamungen and different antagonistic styles of thought. In a word—traditionalism can only become conservatism in a society in which change occurs through the medium of class conflict—in a class society. This is the sociological background of modern conservatism.

Meaning of Radicalism

Radicalism like beauty, is the eye of the beholder. What is considered radical in one context is seen as popular in other. From the view point of Monarchies in Europe and Tories in North America near the end of the 18th century, America represented a radical departure from accepted standards of government. Current communist literature describes America as a prime example of reactionary imperialism. Social reforms policies proposed by Norman Thomas in the 1920's and 1930's in the United States were defined then but are common place now. Abolitionists were radical in the 19th century but are a majority at this time. Free public education was an extreme view in most nations but is now the dominant form of schooling in the most powerful countries. A student labeled radical at a cloistered, quite religious college may be simply another member of a large number of dissenting students at a turbulent, massive state university.

Radical ideas have perplexed, annoyed and changed societies since groups of men have existed. Radicalism is neither an American nor a contemporary trademark. In virtually every society and in each era, men take positions which differ dramatically and extensively from the common view. Sometimes these majority views gain favour and become more generally accepted; at other times the holders of minority views are castigated and persecuted.

Current concern with radical ideas in society and in schools and the social turmoil which may accompany such ideas, gives the misleading impression that radicalism is new and threatening Radical ideas may threaten the precarious stability of societies, but they are not new. Howard Mumford Jones, the distinguished historian, documents the radicalism of early America and points out that the definition of radicalism differs in time, place and prospective. He cites example after example of radical men and ideas from the exploratory period through the radical American Revolution to what he terms the possible twilight of America's radical reputation, the *New Deal* of F.D.R.[14] The revitalization of radicalism in America as both a social and an art form in recent years shows that although the international reputation for radicalism may have passed from the United States, the roots of radicalism run deep and the branches extended throughout century.

It is on these grounds that the study of radical men and ideas is pertinent to an understanding of society and its institutions. No society remains static—all are in varying stages of change, and the dynamics of social change are partly the result of radical views from other times and places. As societies change, so do social institutions. Family, religion, crime, medicine, communications, organizations and education have undergone evolutionary and revolutionary alteration in different societies at different times. Although the impact of a specific radical view on any social institution is difficult to measure, there are significant indications of institutional change related to radical ideas. Social club organization was modified by the prohibition movement. Family structure has been altered by the once radical idea of women suffrage. Religion is being influenced by birth control, abortion, reform and *"God is Dead"* viewpoint. Each of these would have been viewed as extreme heresy in earlier times. Income tax, social security and federal aid to education were radical ideas at their inception.

This is not to say that all radical ideas work or have merit. Indeed, many radical view have been totally ignored, proven unworkable, or thoroughly discounted. *Anarchy* as a political form has never gained many adherents in modern society. After Washington's time proposals to establish an American monarchy have been ignored or denied. There are many radical men and ideas whose contributions cannot even be recalled because they did not achieve notoriety in their own time.

Although radicalism may be merely a label applied to any idea that differs from one's own, a clear statement of the dimensions of radicalism would include the idea of basic opposition to the popular more opinions and values of a given society at a particular time. In these terms, a radical idea would be one that proposes a dramatic or extensive change in a major aspect of the life pattern of any culture.

Radicalism may be viewed as positive or negative depending upon the purposes of those who promote a particular radical doctrine. Negative radicalism preaches the abolition of a presumed major evil in society without offering any particular social alternative.

Those who see capitalism as an evil and propose radical elimination of that economic system without proposing a better one to replace it may be seen as negative radicals. They may speak or act in a manner which is essentially destructive, such as that involved in the bombing of a bank, a business, or a university. A positive radicalism example would be utopian writers who proposes idyllic situations for the good of all men without necessarily castigating the present condition of man. Most radical social theories combine the idea of exorcising evils and substituting utopias and involve, therefore both negative and positive radicalism. The radical view fundamentally assumes that there are basic wrongs in the social system and its institutions and that these require drastic changes in order to produce the better society.

In essence, the radical's views are indirect opposition to the values and customs of his own culture. He desires to change specific conditions in the culture so that the alternative model corresponds to his idealization of a better society. Radicals may be found in many different occupational areas. The thrust of radical ideas may come from an informed student group, a worker's revolt, an organization or an individual. The impact of a particular radical idea varies from no alteration to the initiation of major social changes.

Clinton Rossiter recognized the difficulty in defining terms that have wide public usage but lack precision. He proposed a spectrum of seven "terms" running sequentially as follows revolutionary radicalism, liberalism, conservatism, standpatism, reaction and revolutionary reaction. The basic distinction among them, in Rossiter's view, is their attitude toward change and reform in areas like law, human relations, economics, customs, and education. Radicalism including the revolutionary forms is committed to thorough change. Liberalism, conservatism and standpatism are varieties of attitudes which promote change over stability over change but are relatively content within the existing social system. Reaction and revolutionary reaction are attitudes which Rossiter defines as desiring to change toward the past, relishing earlier times, and willing to act "radically" to return the society to the ideals of a period perceived as superior to the present. The revolutionary aspects of radicalism and reaction exist in the willingness to the use violence if necessary to obtain goals. Rossiter notes the close proximity of radicalism and reaction to each other in terms of specific beliefs and behaviours.[15]

Radical thought and action may be drawn from either end of a spectrum of social and political ideas. The common use of the terms right and left in regard to political, economic, and social thought is modified by adding the term radical. The radical right and radical left are positions of polarity that can be depicted by diagram as follows:

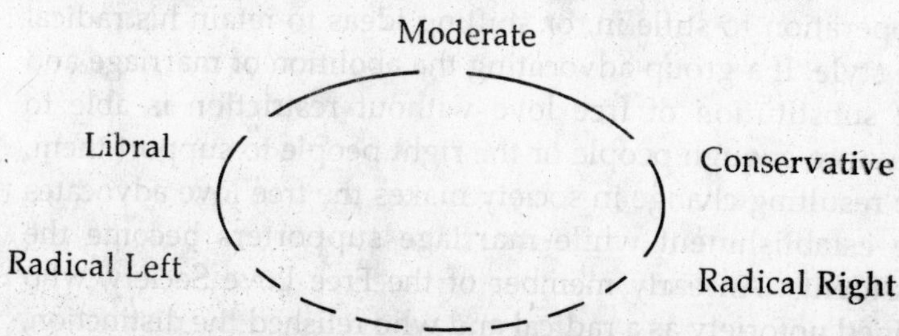

In political science literature, the term *"reactionary"* is used to signify the extreme right and *"radical"* is reserved for the far left. Here, "radical" is used to refer to both ends of spectrum. Both the far right and the far left are in agreement that basic changes are needed to reform existing social institutions. They differ not in their radicalism per sec but in the particular goals or means they view as important for the society. The radical right is a term which may be legitimately used to describe men and ideas of the for right politically.[16]

Radicalism contains the seeds of self destruction. A radical view is necessarily one which is in opposition to a commonly held idea. If the radical view becomes popular or powerful by persuasion or force—it is no longer radical. To the extent that a radical idea is accepted in a society, it changes from radical to moderate. As acceptability increases, radicalism decreases presumably, to goal; of a radical group is to gain power in order to have its radical ideas adopted. The achievement of that goal produces the demise of the group as a radical function.

This is not merely semantic snag resulting from our definition of radicalism. It is important to an understanding of psycho-social dynamics in radicalism. It helps to explain why radicals of one period are moderates of another and vice versa. It also suggests that the processional radical has a difficult time when he begins to develop influence. He needs to choose among alternatives which include social respectability as a result of adoption of his ideas, compromises and modifications in putting the ideas into practice, cooperation to stifle in, or shifting ideas to retain his radical life style. If a group advocating the abolition of marriage and the substitution of free love without restriction is able to convince enough people or the right people to support them, the resulting change in society makes the free love advocates the establishment while marriage supporters become the dissidents. An early member of the Free Love Society, who gained notoriety as a radical and who relished the distinction, must now choose to defend the new establishment, with draw silently, or take up a new cause. Typically, social change is much more complex than the example given, but the concept of successful radicalism being self-destroying is a useful perspective.

Walter Weyt discusses aspects of this weakness in radical movements. He describes two groups of radical: those by environment and those by temperament. He argues that a radical by environment is slower but more sure, while a radical by temperament is faster, more violent, and less realistic. It is the latter, contents Weyt, *"who fades quickest when his emotions are forsaken for the emotional behaviour"*. An environmental radical however, draw from the conditions of life to which he has been subjected and has more staying power. Weyt also writes about the relation of age to radicalism, proposing that the period of adolescence *"is the true day for revolt"*. While age brings pleasant spouses, self indulgence, and expertise in why "every thing is impossible".[17]

Radicalism, then has several dimensions. It is conditioned by time and space. Radical ideas are those that fundamentally conflict with popular ideas. Radicalism can incorporate destructive, utopian or combination positions. Radicals may be those who supports a radical idea in one or more spheres of life but needn't be totally opposed to all aspects. Not all radical ideas gain supporters. For the few that develop public notoriety, many feisty to attract general attention. And the radical ideas that becomes popularly accepted is no longer a radical idea.

There is a current tendency to equate radicals with violence. Although physical violence is a radical act in a society which formerly outlaws such behaviour, it does not follow that violence is the only form of radicalism. Some might note that violence is a general social condition and therefore, not radical. Regardless of whether violence is seen as radical or non-radical, these are other acts which are radicals but not violent. *Passive resistance and peaceful civil disobedience as advocated by Gandhi,* Thoreau and Martin Luther King *represent radical behaviour which is non-violent.* Living in communes, existing without modern technology or engaging in Satan worship are other examples or radical behaviour that needn't be violent.

Recent reports have documented the extent and tradition of violence in American life, most notably the report of Hugh Davis Graham and Ted Robert Gurr[18] and the task force report directed by Jerome H. Skolnick.[19] Both documents were submitted to the National Commission on the causes and prevention of violence and posit that violence has long been one form of American protest behaviour. This does not make it more or less radical than peaceful acts of protest on the espousal of radical ideas. Violence is dramatic and public, leading to a common assumption that radicalism and violence are virtually synonymous. It is true that some radicals advocate violence and that violence may result from belief in certain radical values, but there is no necessary correlation between physical destruction and radical thought.

In addition, it might be useful to delineate radical behaviour from radical thought. In practice the two may coincide, but it is possible to consider radical ideas outside of individual radical behaviour. A person may advocates the abolition of government while personally accepting the rewards and personality of a government. Marshal McLuhan proposes a radically different way of viewing environment which suggests that printing is outmoded but he does in printed books.[20] There is also adequate evidence of people who engage in radical behaviour without obvious radical thought. A sexual deviate may not have considered a relational for his behaviour, but seeks gratification merely as a physical act. An *eccentric* who carries a bag of leaves around town may have no thoughtful radical purpose or design. A sniper shooting at students on a campus may be emotionally disturbed but not a follower of some radical ideology.

Radical ideas are usually expressed to stimulate action and change behaviour. Solid and consistent logic, emotional barrages of fiery rhetoric and persuasive examples of goodness or evil are utilized to convince people to become believers, advocates and practitioners, regardless of the immediate behavioural.

Consequence of radical view points, the idea themselves considered. This intellectual tradition of radicalism has been the subject or many writers. The *"Radical Republic"* of eighteenth century America described by Mumford Jones incorporated aspects of both right and left wing thinking. He identified the British philosopher Edmund Burke and the American pamphleteer Thomas Paine as representatives of the radical right and the radical left respectively.

T.B. Bottomore glances briefly at social criticism in classical Rome and Greece and settles on the age of enlightenment as the beginning of Western radical thought. Bottomore's essays treat contemporary radical thought in the United States and Canada as well as the their European counterparts.

A special meaning for the term radical as it relates to the contemporary student movement is suggested by Harold Taylor his concept is that a radical is one who makes judgements about qualities of life in term of experience and consequences rather than by reference to authority ideology. Ideological considerations in politics, religion and economies however have provided impetus to the radical right in America. David H. Bennett analyses four *"radicals of the right"* and their movement during the depression. His treatment of Father Charles Conghlin, Rev. Gerald L.K. Smith, Dr. Francis E. Townsend, and representative William Lemke and the union party shows the use of fundamentalist religious doctrine, anti-communism, and economic utopias in forging an intense political campaign.

Radical ideas have long and colourful stories. The dynamics of social provide constant opportunities for expressions of unorthodox use. Periods of crisis after more compelling environments for movements demagogues, rash behaviour, and rapid communication of radical thoughts, but the intellectual rules of radicalism reside in the considered judgment of those who reflect on the human condition.

Radical social ideas have the potential for influencing socially expected thought and behaviour, they are appropriate subjects of study for those interested in social change. The transactional concept of social process which assumes that change in one segment or institution of society results from an effect change in other segments, makes a broad study of social ideas—radical and moderate—necessary. The presumably radical idea of a guaranteed annual ways does not simply form welfare bureaus, nor will it only effect present welfare recipients. The old debtor's prisons, free medical clinic facilities, religious charities and preachings, social concepts of qualities and hard works, competitions based economics, free schooling and mass media advertising each contribute to a well being effected to changes inherent in the radical idea. Even if a specific radical idea is not successful it may stimulate social institutions or individual, to non radical change to the extent that an radical idea has public notoriety, it presents an environment for social and institutional modification.

This does not once again mean that any notorious radical idea will produce a change in its favour. In fact the radical ideas also produce alterations in opposition to the idea. A radical proposal to permit the sale of hard drugs in school and colleges as a connivance to students would cause reconsideration of drug abuse problems in colleges and schools and might change regulations to be more strict in surveillance searches and reporting of drug use. The point is that the radical ideas if adequately disseminated assist in the determination of policies and practices of institutions and their societies.

Education, both formal as in schooling and informal as in life experiences, is an social institution sharing in society and participating in the transactional process. Radical ideas, in society in other social institution and in regard to education itself has the potential of the great or modest change in the way we think about colleges, students, teachers, curriculum. Mass free public education was a radical idea earlier times it did not developed spontaneously from school masters and professors and its effects have not been limited to what goes on during college hours. Major social ideas about equality, participating citizenship, labour and economics, industrial development, child welfare, class struggles and human nature contributed to and have been influenced by mass education.

Educational institutions have emerged as major social institutions involving virtually every person for stained periods of time in generally prescribed activities. The basic purpose and fancy deemed appropriate by those in educational power school and colleges incorporate the dominant norms and values of their societies and engaged in the socialization process to produce citizens with similar beliefs.

This social stability function of educational institution in highly consistent with their role as reflectors of society and maintenance of the culture. Often times educational institutions are even more conservative in their pattern of change then the general society because they are perceived as the protectors of the past. Hair length regulations have changed more slowly, and frequently with greater institutional reluctance, in educational institutions than in many other areas of society. Citizen rights to fee expression assembly, and due process are continually challenged in schools because of Social questions about the citizenship of students. Teachers are still being fired or resigned for rising questions about the norms and values of the society. None in recent times has met the fate of Socrates, who challenged the popular ideas of his time and was condemned to die for corrupting the morals of Youth, but many have felled a similar worth from the society. As an education was met by a radical response Socrates resulting in death.[21]

The reflective, protective, status quo education system is consistent with aspects of socialization that call for non=critical assimilation of the traditions and mores of a society inconsistent with the dynamics of an open society based on enlightened citizens and persistent change. Radical ideas, are worthy of consideration not because they are good ideas, but because they are ideas-and ideas are the means for virtuality in a dynamic society.

Higher educational institutions have been remiss in providing opportunities for those going into teaching to grapple with radical social ideas and to see educational implications. Seldom are these students, who will become educational decision-marks in public and private educational institutions, asked to consider dissident viewpoints in their own education. It would be unlikely that teachers who are unaware of radical positions would be able to introduce their students to new ideas, while it is time that many colleges expect their teacher-education students to examine radical school ideas, it is unusual for them to undertake study of the inter-relationships between radical social thought and the educational institutions.

Today our country is facing a critical period in its history and that account everybody concerned with education has a responsibility for knowing what he is trying to do in bringing up the next generation and why he is trying to do. The country is faced with a very severe challenge in the shape of various economic, social and moral changes and its future depends on the response we make to this challenge. A society that strives to improve as it changes becomes keenly aware of its social problems. We live in a such society, social problems seems deceptively easy to understand when compared to physical or biological problems.

Social problems are behaviour patterns or conditions that are considered objectionable and desirable by many members of a society. The members recognize that corrective policies, programs and services are necessary to cope with the reduce the scope of these problems. All social problems are analyzed from the view point of sociology which has a find of knowledge about them consequently these problems are analyzed in terms of group processes and social relationships.

Through education we can remove evil and problems of society. In removing these evils, teachers play pivotal role and hence they are called *"agent of social change."* The behaviour of teachers greatly influenced the students so it is essential that a teacher should have open minded and radical at time. Teaching has a pivotal place in molding a civilized society. Right from the beginning of civilization teaching profession has been regarded as the noblest profession. It has striven to fulfill the ultimate aim of creating a sober and healthy society by lying a firm foundation of character building, social efficiency, spread of national culture and happiness.

"The strength of a nation", writes Moffitt, is largely dependent upon the kind and amount of education of its people.[22] Education in any country reflects the needs and aspirations of its people. These needs and aspirations are never static because the new environmental forces bring about constant change in life and ideals of society. The increasing complexity of modern life brings growing insistence on more and more effective education. Education is considered a principal factor of social change. *"Teaching"* as Mr. Joad says, "is not everybody's cup of tea". Teacher is a source of dynamic force for all the teaching learning activities.

Apart from imparting knowledge to the pupil, he influences them in difficult ways. The teacher acts as a pivot for the transmission of intellectual technical skills and cultural tradition from one generation to the other. The teacher who is the architect of the new generation has to mould the mind and chisel the behaviour of the young.

A true teacher instead of feeling bored by daily routine will rather evil himself by constant practice. A teacher in the true sense of the term is a transforming personality. Rightly it has been remarked that the teacher is not an instructor or a task master but a helper and a guide. His business is to guide and not to impose. He does bring perfection of the pupils mind he only shows him how to perfect his instruments of knowledge and helps and encourages him in a process.

Until the advent of Scientific method and rise of social sciences, social problems were not very much recognized and occasionally taken for granted At best social issues were dealt with by arm-chair thinkers. As a result the course of society could not be very much controlled whatever direction there was to social process, it was to a set of rigid formalities which were not scientifically examined. The time has come to when both in the developing and advanced cultures there is a great need to study factors which retard or accelerate social change. In the developing countries overweighed with age-old and unexamined traditions with the attendant consequences of confusion and cultural inertia, it is imperative that scientific study be directed to the problem of social change.

In India we are presently passing through a crucial period of social change as never before. Old social order is being challenged by the new modes of life. Cormack (1968), did research on Indian College and University students' conscious awareness of and attitude towards social change related to "traditional", India becoming "Modern". On the basis of her research she concluded that "Social change is taking place more rapidly than most realize." In understanding this confrontation of the old and the new and in solving new and complex problem of our time we have to change our personality outfit considerably. Kuppuswamy and Mehta (1968), discussing that the transformation of Indian Society from a traditional to a modern one say, *"The involves not only enormous economic changes but also a basic change in the personality structure of individual from a dependent to an autonomous person." "In a country where tradition extending to thousands of years of the primitive past are controlling the behaviour of the mass, you cannot except to push the most uptodate sociopolitical ideas without changing the existing attitudes and mental makeup of people."* (Rath and Mishra, 1963)

The values and behaviour of the pupils are influenced by a number of factors teachers being one of them. The teachers play a very important role in the development of their pupils. The teachers educate the pupils and try to make them modern. But some times we see that these agents of social change, communicators of new knowledge and transmitter of culture are also involved in conservatism. They look conservative in their personal, social and religious area of life. The present study is intended to know whether the teachers are more conservative or radical in their life. It becomes necessary too, for the social scientist (and being teacher in a degree college) to measure the behaviour pattern of teachers on the scale of conservatism and radicalism.

REFERENCES

1. John C. Moffit, In *Science Education for Teachers*. Washington D.C.: The Centre for Applied Research in Education, 1963, p. 7.
2. Mukherji, S.N., *Secondary School Administration*, Acharya Book Depot, Baroda, 1959, p. 10.
3. Gibran, Khalil, *The Prophet: William Human*, L.T.P. Maltomume London (1956 Edition).
4. Shamuddin Raipur, Teachers as builders of a new nation. *Progress of Education*. Vol. LIX, No. 8, March 1985, p. 189.
5. K.G. Saiyedain, *Problem of Educational Reconstruction*, Bombay, Asia Publishing, 1950.
6. Cf. Lord Hugh Cecil, *Conservatism*, Home University Library of Modern Knowledge, pp. 9f. New York and London.
7. *Ibid.*, p. 2.
8. C.f. The Article "Konservative" by Rackfahl in politisches Handworterbuch ed: P. Herre Leipzig, 1923.
9. *Ibid.*

10. C.f. Lord Hugh Cecil, *op. cit.*, p. 64.
11. Cf. L. Bergstrasser, 'Geschichte der politischen Partein in Deutschland' Schiftenseihe der Verraltungsakademie Berlin, No. 42nd Ed. p. 5, Mannheim Berlin and Leipzig.
12. In Medieval times too, there existed progressive centres, bearers of a dynamic principle. The towns. They were however isolated within static world. So far as we can see the international culture of the Middle Ages, as represented by the church lack this element 'oriented change' in which every event assumes a function effecting the whole. On the difficulties of forming parties in a feudal world, of K. Laperecht. Deutsche Geschichte, Suppl. II, second half volume, p. 53 Freiburg in Breisgau, 1904.
13. Cf. Emil Lederer, 'Das Okonomische Element und die politische 1 dee im modernen parteiwesen, in Zeitechrift for politik, Vol. 5, p.11. Intellectual life in Germany is definitely split up into a liberal and conservative current only after 1840.
14. Howard Mumford Jones, *O Strange New World*, New York: The Viking Press, 1964.
15. Clinton Rossiter, *Conservatism in America: The Thankless Persuasion*, Second Edition, New York: Vintage Books, 1962.
16. Daniel Bell, *The Radical Right*, Garden City, New York: Anchor Books, 1963.
17. Walter Weyl, *Tired Radicals and Other Papers*, New York, B. W. Huebsch, Inc., 1921.
18. Hugh Graham and Ted Robert Gurr, *The History of Violence in America*, New York, 1969.
19. Jerone H. Skolnick, *The Politics of Protest*, New York: Simon and Schuster, 1969.
20. Marshall MacLuhan, *Understanding Media*, New York: 1964.
21. B. Jowett, *The Dialogues of Plato*, Vol. 1, New York: Random House, 1937.
22. John C. Moffitt, *In Science Education for Teachers*, Washington D.C. The Centre for Applied Research in Education, 1963, p.7.

Chapter 2

Review of Related Studies

As early as 1925, Moore submitted Rice's conservatism-radicalism scale to a class of 225 students. He failed to find any differences among radicals and conservatives in regard to intellectual level and emotional stability measured by Woodworth P. D. form. The study revealed that radicals have a few stronger traits like greater speed of reaction, ease of breaking habits, readiness to make snap judgments and independence in that face of majority influences as compared to conservatives. Radicals were better in thinking in thousand terms and give fewer common response than the conservative. In contrast, a conservative subordinates his conduct to the prevalent standard.

Vetter (1930-31), investigated the relationship of socio-political attitudes and various personality traits by giving a number of tests i.e., *Sheet Thorndike Intelligence Examination, Ottis Advanced Examination, Allport A. S. Test, Larisd C_2 Test, Kent Rosanoff Test, and Suggestibility Test* to, 1,200 University students. As compared to the conservatives, radicals were found to the superior in intelligence more introverted and having greater individualization. Radical women proved to the more ascendant than the conservative one.

Dexter (1938-39), threw some light on the problem by administering Lentz C.R. Opinioaire to 267 students. A variety of other test were given i.e., *Bernrenter Personality Inventory Henmon-Nelson test of Mental Ability.*

Morris Trait Index and Downey Will Temperament Test. A positive correlation was found ranging from 0.20 to 0.35 between radicalism and intelligence, introversion, self-sufficiency, general information and dominance. Negative correlation ranging from 0.20 to 0.35 were found between radicalism and speed of decision and movement.

Sanai and Pickard (1949), attacked the problem by posing this question *"Is there sufficient experimental support to disprove the hypothesis of nil-relationship between radicalism and personality traits"*. With this end in view a test of politico-economic radicalism-conservatism was conducted. It was given to a group of 70 women students in a private London Training college. Age range was between 19-24 years. Along with it were given an intelligence test and Roschach Test Scores on intelligence, radicalism, Roschach test, and rating by a lecturer on seven tests were inter-correlated. On the basis of Roschach test and ratings by a lecturer, radicalism was found to be correlated with emotionally (0.020, - 0.19) emotional control (0.009, 0.15), cheerfulness (0.078, 0.07), aggression (0.04, 0.14), integration (0.031, 0.01), and intelligence (0.248, 0.025) correlation (based on Roschach Test) between intelligence and radicalism supports the previous studies. None of the other previously traits seemed to be correlated with radicalism. Radicalism - introversion is the highest and might be higher if correlated.

One of the pioneering work in this field has been done by Adonio *et al.* (1950). The research reported in this volume was guided by the following major hypothesis that the political economic, and social convictions of an individual after form a brand coherent pattern, as if bound together by a "mentality" or "spirit" and that this pattern is an expression of deep-lying trends in his personality.

Dreger (1952), concluded a study with various Church groups as subjects. Ferguson Scale (Religious attitude)

Wonderlic personal test (intelligence), Rozenweing picture frustration study TAT, and Rorschach tests were administered. The investigator noted that in the area of perpetual keenness and insight liberals are more developed than conservatives. These differences can be used as a suggestive hypothesis for further research. Conservatives have greater need for dependence and liberals are more independents.

Eysenck (1954), too did research in this field. He accepted provisionally the view that tender mindedness and tough mindedness are not in themselves representatives of attitude constellations, but rather the projection of personality variables on to a Radical-Conservative attitude continue. Further results show that there is a close relationship between tough-mindedness and extroversion on the hand and between tender mindedness and introversion on the other. Three experimental proofs were given all of which verified this hypothesis.

Newcomb (1957), made a valuable contribution in this field. He received the question *"What kinds of personal characteristics in any student community determine these social relationships which in turn, head to varying reactions to proposed social changes?"* The study makes use of these major types of data, paper and pencil questionnaire responses, written reports on individual students filled in college officers, and individual interviews.

McClosky (1958), on the basis of PAR study carried out on the sample of 1,211 persons, obtained similar kind of results as crutch field. He concluded that conservative beliefs are more frequently found in the unformed, the poorly educated, and the less intelligent conservatives and liberals are found to be sharply distinguished on clinical-personality variables. The figures demonstrate with overpowering effect that conservatives tend to serve on the more undesirable, poorly adapted side of personality variables. The extreme conservatives are easily the most hostile suspicious, the most rigid and compulsive.

Similarly, in the quest of finding relationship between conservatism and various personality traits, Photiadis (1962), found that the following results, using a sample of 300 adult men and women who are members of three Protestant churches, conservatism was found to be related to orthodoxy (0.75), extrinsic-intrinsic values (0.443), Anomie (414), status concern (0.572) Authoritarianism (0.497), withdrawal tendencies (0.216), multi-social tendencies (0.253), and education (0.080).

Boarding (1963) administered questionnaires to 192 college students varying in age and background. Scores on radicalism scale (included in Cattel's 16 p. questionnaire) were correlated with the following personality scales (i) MPI, (ii) Taylor's manifest anxiety scale; (iii) California F scale; and (iv) Base social acquiescence scale. The result did not show any significant correlation between radicalism and extroversion on anxiety. Low negative correlation's were found between radicalism neuoticism and California Authoritarianism scale. Radicalism was negatively correlated (0.32) with Base Acquiescence scale for women.

A study by Mittal (1965), on 50 women showed a positive relationship between conservatism and neuroticism, a negative relationship between convertism and dominance. In brief, the progressive ones, were found to be introverted lacking Self-sufficiency, submissive and displaying clear cut neurotic trends.

Suma Chitnis (1973-74) investigated into the role of college teachers in the college system by undertaking an analysis of their status and their functioning at three colleges affiliated to Bombay University. The social background of the these teachers, their performance, their relationship and role conflict are described and an examination of the level of their professionalisation, their unionization, their commitment to and outlook upon higher education in general and to the academic profession in particular. She points out that 'research' into the social backgrounds, attitudes, values, achievements, aspirations and pattern of behaviour of students and of teachers seems to have been the most popular theme for research.

In her recent *Trend Report on the Sociology of Education in India* Suma Chitnis explains, that *'The research and writing on college teachers in more extensive than the research and writing on school teachers'*. (Chitnis, 1985, p. 223)

Similar issues were studied by Jayaram and Sivarama Krishnan (1976), and Ramanamma (1979), with respect to academics working in Bangalore University and University of Poona, respectively.

Altbach (1977, 1979), dwells upon the problem of ambivalence among college teachers in India. He observes that there is *"confusion about the appropriateness of some expectations are not being met, and an understanding that the realities of college teaching are not appropriate to the great academic traditions."* He adds that the factors which contribute to this feeling of ambivalence are inadequate remuneration, poor working conditions, lack of autonomy in goal setting and work related activity, severe constraints on innovations in teaching evaluation.

Herdia (1979a), is concerned with the socio-demographic profile of college teachers. He examined how far socio-demographic profile supports the image of academician as modernizing elites in Third World. This study was based on an extensive survey of arts and science college in Bombay city conducted during 1976-77. Herdia (1979b), is concerned with the process of decision-making. He takes into account two dimensions of decision-making process; the distribution of authority and the criteria of decision-making. The analysis of the distribution of authority is based on the actual pattern of exercised influence rather than official structure of formal authority distribution with a low level of influence of faculty members in the colleges. Thus among the criteria for decision making, there is a consistent prominence to bureaucratic criteria while professional criteria are weighted rather low.

Yogendra Singh (1979), examines the role of teachers of Rajasthan University as agents of change. He focuses on measurement of the levels of modernization, aspiration, commitment, moral and authoritarianism among the teachers. The role structure of university teachers has been assessed through a combination of data on the above variables.

Another area of research in higher education has been that of teachers organization. This aspect has been the subject of study of scholars like Browne (1976), Clark (1977), Coates (1972), Cole (1969), Deem (1976), Duke (1973), Manzer (1970) and Mortimer and Lozier (1972). It may be mentioned here that this area of research in India has been rather neglected by scholars. Jayaraman and Sivaramakrishnan (1979), discuss faculty unionism with special reference to college teachers in Bangalore University in the state of Karnataka. They examine the nature and function of teachers organizations, perspective of their organizations developing into a movement and the implications of these for the professionalisation of teaching.

Eisemen (1974), examined the impact of exposure to American Universities on teachers at engineering colleges and I.I.T.'s in India. Eisenmen and Ghosh (1979), examine some of the institutional influences on the professional out look and behaviour among engineering faculty in India.

Discussing about the personality patterns of conservative McClosky (1958), to say that, "*in many ways hostility is a principal component of the conservative personality... conservatives prefer to believe in man's wickedness... expressed as political doctrine, these projections of aggressive personality tendencies take on the respectability of an old and honoured philosophical position. These tendencies may also lie at the root of conservative will not violate the conditions necessary for the order, to train him to value duty, obedience and conformity, property church and the family. The high values placed on authority, leadership, and natural hierarchy, and on an elite to guide and check the rest of mankind apparently derive from the same set of psychological impulses.*"

Photladis (1962), found conservatives to be having anti-social tendencies. Krout and Stagner (1939), found radicals to be handicapped in social relations. McNamra and Darley

(1938), found correlation ranging from 0.36 to 0.46 between general adjustment as measured by Bell inventory and economic conservatism.

Promila Vasudeva (1976), had examined a sample of post-graduate students and their personality traits in relation to their general attitude towards social change and in particular whether their outlook will be conservative or radical. The conclusions arrived at are based on a scientific application of scale product method covering attitudes in six areas of social change viz., marriage, technology, education, women place in Indian society, religion and tradition. The investigator had found that radicalism is positively correlated with 14 of the 17 traits chosen for the study which argues will for social change drawing support better equipped in personality traits like confidence, intelligence, responsibility, flexibility, social presence and desire for achievement. All the above studies are related to the assessment of personality and attitudes as more submitted rice conservatism - radicalism scale to a class of 225 students but he failed to find the any differences among radicals and conservatives. Vetter investigated the relationship of socio-cultural attitudes and various personality traits by giving a number of tests i.e socio cultural attitude scale. Newcomb, Bending and P.V. Vasudeva all had examined the students and their personality traits with reference to radical and conservative attitudes.

But the present study is related to the teachers' behaviours in sociological contexts, those who are torch bearer, a guide and a transmitter of culture. A teacher who is the architect of the new generation has to mould the mind and chisel the attitude of the young. Education is a comprehensive and synthetic process which aims at harmonious development of the body, mind, emotion and spirit of the talent of the student. The values attitudes of the pupils are influenced by a number of factors—teachers being one of them.

It becomes necessary for the social scientist and being a teacher to measure the behaviour pattern of teachers on the scale of conservatism and radicalism. In the present study the investigator has assessed the behaviour and attitude of university and college teachers with respect to their personal, social and religious areas of life. A five point scale has been applied to assess the attitude of sample teachers from University and its affiliated college teachers with respect to their age, qualification, sex and three areas of life namely personal, social and religious.

Chapter 3

Research Methodology

The present investigation was conducted mainly to find the Lucknow University and it associated degree college teacher's behaviour towards radicalism and conservatism. In case it was required to obtain a global picture of teachers (Professors, Readers, Lecturers) behaviour. But here the purpose was limited only to the testing of behaviour and attitude mainly personal, social and religious areas of life. In this sociological study one attempt has been made to see effect of sex, age, educational qualifications, family backgrounds, activism, political background, professional organization of the Professors, Readers and Lecturers on their behaviour pattern and attitudes towards radicalism and conservatism.

Following are the data of Professors, Readers and Teachers of Lucknow University and its Associated Degree College Teachers.

All the teachers or subject belonged from two areas.

(1) Lucknow University.

(2) Associated Degree colleges.

First of them, the data of Lucknow University is given below:

Faculty	*Professors*		*Readers*		*Lecturers*		*Total*	
Numbers	*Male*	*Female*	*Male*	*Female*	*Male*	*Female*	*Male*	*Female*
6	47	3	25	25	25	25	97	53

The data of Associated Degree College Teachers of Lucknow University is given in the table below.

Total No. of Degree Colleges	*Total No. of Depart-ments*	*Teachers*				*Total*	*Total*	
		Readers		*Lecturers*				
		Male	*Female*	*Male*	*Female*		*Male*	*Female*
6	62	40	35	40	35	150	80	70
						75 Readers 75 Lecturers		

The present chapter deals with the description of methods adopted in carrying out this investigation and procedures followed in selection of samples, the tools of study, collection of data.

It is necessary that objectives of the present study should be clear before adopting the above cited methods and procedure.

The objectives of present study have been formulated under the following points:

1. To study Lucknow University and its associated college teachers' behaviour at the scale of radicalism and conservatism.
2. To find out a comparative analysis between male and female teacher regarding conservatism and radicalism in their personal, social and religious areas of life.
3. To assess Lucknow University and its associated college teachers' attitude towards radicalism and conservatism.

Following are the hypothesis of the present study.

(1) There is a difference between male and female teacher towards conservatism and radicalism.

(2) There are some personality traits to establish the relationship between conservatism and radicalism.

(3) There is no difference between university and college teachers behaviour towards conservatism and radicalism with respect to their sex.

(4) There is no difference between male and female teacher's attitude towards conservatism and radicalism on the basis of their personal social and religious areas of life.

DESCRIPTION OF THE SAMPLE

The subject for the study was Lucknow University and its associated degree college teacher's behaviour towards radicalism and conservatism.

Teachers to be classified are male and female into two categories. The study had covered three areas of life these being personal area, social area and economic area. Male and female teachers of Lucknow University and its associated degree colleges were classified according to their age, religion and caste designation (Rank), educational qualification and family composition also because the study has been analysed on these basis.

Total sample size of the study was three hundred (300) one hundred seventy seven (177). Male teachers, 97 from University level and 80 from degree college level and one hundred twenty three (123) female teachers, 53 from University level and 70 from degree college level were taken for the present study. The study has covered 6 faculty and 27 departments from the Lucknow University and 6 associated degree colleges for the present study. The study was done on the basis of sex with respect to age, qualification, rank, religion, caste and family composition etc. of Lucknow University and its associated degree college teachers to find out the results of their personal, social and religious areas of life.

All the teachers or subject belonged from two levels. These levels are:

1. Lucknow University, Lucknow

2. Associated degree colleges of Lucknow University.

(1) Lucknow University

One hundred and fifty teachers were taken from twenty seven departments of Lucknow University. The data is given below:

S. No.	*Department*	*Professors*		*Readers*		*Lecturers*		*Total*
		Male	*Female*	*Male*	*Female*	*Male*	*Female*	
1.	English	1	–	1	1	1	2	6
2.	Philosophy	1	–	1	1	1	2	6
3.	Psychology		3	–	2	1	1	7
4.	History	2	–	2		1	–	5
5.	Pol. Science	1	–	2	1	1	–	5
6.	Public Adm.	1	–	1	–	1	–	3
7.	Economics	2	–	1		1	–	4
8.	Social Work	2	–	1	1	–	1	5
9.	Arabic	1	–	–		1	–	2
10.	Persian	1	–	1	1	1	–	4
11.	Hindi	2	–	1	2	1	1	7
12.	Linguistic	1	–	–	–	1	–	2
13.	Physics	4	–	–	3	1	1	9
14.	Chemistry	4	–	1	2	1	2	9
15.	Bio-Chemistry	5	–	–	–	1	1	7
16.	Botany	4	–	1	2	1	2	10
17.	Geology	3	–	–	1	1	2	7
18.	Zoology	2	–	1	2	1	3	9
19.	Mathematics	1	–	2	–	2	–	5
20.	Statistics	4	–	1	–	2	1	8
21.	Law Faculty	1	–	2	–	2	–	5
22.	Education	2	–	–	3	–	3	8
23.	Commerce	1	–	1	1	1	–	4
24.	Anthropology	1	–	1	2	–	1	5
25.	Sociology	–	–	1	–	–	1	2
26.	Urdu	–	–	1	–	–	1	2
27.	Business Admn.	–	–	2	–	1	–	3
	Total	47	3	25	25	25	25	

(2) Degree Colleges:

Six Degree Colleges from Lucknow city were taken for the study. These degree colleges are:

S. No.	*Degree Colleges*	*Department -Number*	*Readers Male*	*Readers Female*	*Lecturers Male*	*Lecturers Female*	*Total*
1.	Christian College, Lucknow	8	18	2	16	8	44
2.	I.T. Degree College, Lucknow	10	2	3	2	2	9
3.	Karamat Husain Post Graduate College, Lucknow	12	–	10	–	5	15
4.	Khun Khunji Mahila Vidyalya, Lucknow.	9	–	10	–	5	15
5.	Mahila Vidyalya Lucknow	11	2	5	2	10	19
6.	Shia Post Graduate College, Lucknow	12	18	5	20	5	48
	Total	62	40	35	40	35	150

Twenty seven departments of Lucknow University and six degree college of the Lucknow city were selected for the present study. One hundred fifty (150) teachers from Lucknow and 150 teachers from degree colleges were taken from three faculties i.e. Science, Arts and Commerce. The researcher collected the data of Professors only from Lucknow University but Readers and Lecturers were available from both levels (University and college).

For the study of male and female teachers of Lucknow University and its associated degree college teachers behaviour towards radicalism and conservatism on the basis of age the teachers were classified into different categories of age group the minimum age group was 20 years and the maximum age group was 55.

To study the male and female teachers of Lucknow University and its associated degree colleges on the basis of their designation the teachers were also classified into three categories: from university level—Professors, Readers and Lecturers were taken for the present investigation and from degree college level Readers and Lecturers were taken to assess the objectives of the study. The present study has covered three areas of life namely—personal, social and religious.

For the study of male and female teachers of Lucknow University and its associated degree college teachers on the basis of their educational qualification the teachers were taken from three faculties-Arts faculty, Science faculty and Commerce faculty. All teachers' last qualification were noted for the study and extra-qualifications were also noted for the study.

For the study of male and female teachers' economic position the investigator has taken the monthly income of Professors, Readers and Lecturers.

For the study of male and female teachers' behaviour and attitude towards radicalism and conservatism on the basis of family background, the teachers were classified into joint and nuclear family background.

For the analysis of male and female Lucknow University and its associated degree college teachers' behaviour towards radicalism and conservatism in these areas of life namely personal, social and religious, the teachers were classified into two groups—male and female.

The present study is a sociological study and the universe of the study is Lucknow University and its associated degree college teachers. To assess the teachers behaviour these areas were covered by the investigator to find out the scientific result:

(1) Family background and family education.

(2) Professional organizational setup.

(3) Activism.

(4) Political background.

To assess the Lucknow University and its associated teachers' attitude towards radicalism and conservatism a five point scale is administered with respect to their personal, social and religious area of life. A five point scale is used for scoring the attitude scale in following manner.

5 marks	Fully agree
4 marks	Agree
3 marks	Undecided
2 marks	Disagree
1 marks	Fully disagree.

Radical conservative attitude scale by L. N. Dubey is used by the investigator to assess the university and Degree college teachers' attitude towards radicalism and conservatism. The scale consists of 60 items, depicted in question which covered three areas—personal social and religious. Each area has 20 items i.e. 20 questions are related to personal area of life, 20 questions are related to the social area of life and 20 questions to the religious area of life. This radical and conservative attitude scale is constructed with an objective to discriminate radicalism and conservatism.

The universe of my research was Lucknow University and its associated college teachers. The present investigation was based on exploratory and formulative research design. The stratified random sampling on three level—Professors, Readers and Lecturers were used proportionate to deduct the sample of 300 teachers from the Lucknow University and its associated degree colleges. Primary and secondary sources of data were used. In primary sources specially the method interview schedule was adopted and in secondary sources books, Journals, magazines and pertinent literature regarding the research were also used.

A questionnaire schedule was administered for the Study, which has covered the Bio-data of the teachers, family background, personal and family educational background, Professional organizational setup, activism, political background of the teachers from Lucknow University and its associated degree college.

THE ADMINISTRATION AND DATA COLLECTION

The present study started with the main object of investigating Lucknow University and its associated degree college teachers' behaviour towards conservatism and radicalism in three areas of life—personal, social and religious. The preliminary sample consisted of three hundred teachers from 27 departments of University and 6 associated degree college of the Lucknow University (Art, Science & Commerce faculty).

The scoring format prepared by the investigator to determine and to place them in order. This format is administered in a simple way. For the findings of the result the investigator has analysed the Bio-data of the teachers from the University and its associated degree colleges on the basis of their sex, qualification, rank, economic background, family composition and personal academic career.

In order to collect the data of the present study of University teachers and degree college teachers the interview schedule is used. This schedule consisting of:

(1) Bio-data of teachers (Professors, Readers, Lecturers both male and female)

(2) Family background of teachers and their educational qualification.

(3) Professional organizational setup.

(4) Activism of the teachers.

(5) Political background of the teachers.

(6) Conservative Radical attitude scale.

The data was collected through the field survey. The interview schedule was used for the study. The filling in of schedule was preceded by verbal instruction (besides the instructions printed on the group front page) given by the investigator to the respondents which are as follows.

"I am trying to find out as to what the teachers feel and think about a number of social issues which are important for the society. I am sure, you will find my schedule interesting. You will find in it many questions you have taught about or read in newspapers and magazines or heard on radio and T.V. This schedule will be used for academic purpose only. The best answer is your personal opinion. If any of the statements or meaning of the words are not clear, please feel free to ask me."

A five point is used by the investigator for scoring the conservative radical attitude of the teachers, five points are given to the fully agree, five points to agree, three points to undecided statements, two points to disagree and one point for fully disagree statements has been given by L. N. Dubey in his attitude scale is also given by the investigator in the present study.

In the manual L. N. Dubey has given the range scores of radicals and conservative, male and female, hence through the manual we can divide male and female teachers into five categories either they highly radical, radical, moderate, conservative or highly conservative.

Chapter 4

Presentation and Analysis of Data

The teachers who is the architect of the new generation has to mould the mind and chisel the behaviour of the youth. University and degree level teacher is a source of dynamic force for all the social activities. Building and equipment are important so as curricular and books, but in absence of an genuine teacher all these things prove meaningless.

Teaching has pivot place in moulding a civilized society. Right from the beginning of civilization teaching profession has been regarded as the noblest profession. It has to strive to fulfill the ultimate aim of creating a sober and a healthy society by laying a foundation of character building, social efficiency, spread of national culture and happiness.

The role of higher education and teachers in a society is well known to one and all. The nation's well being depends on the teachers' well being, even though the converse may not be the position in all the cases. The values behaviour pattern and attitudes of the students are influenced by a number of factors, teachers being one of them. The university and college teachers are more important than the other teachers because their students are generally more attached to them emotionally as well as psychologically. The university teachers play a very important role in the development of student. Teacher educate the pupil and try to make them modern.

The present study is concerned only with the study of university and college teachers' behaviour and attitude. In the first phase of the research, after identifying the departments and associated degree colleges, a sample was conducted in order to get some basic information such as university departments numbers and degree colleges of the Lucknow city. The most important of all of them was Lucknow University and associated degree college teachers cooperation and their suggestions.

Through these basic information the investigator had collected the data of present study easily.

ANALYSIS AND INTERPRETATION OF RESULTS

Facts are like birds, they require a string to hold them together, to connect them. But if there is not string, if there is no unifying idea, then even the most distinguished authorities can not help producing unsatisfactory work. (Werner Sombart).

The analysis of data was done to study the tabulated material by breaking parts and putting them together into new arrangements for inferring the tenability of hypothesis formulated.

It is essentially involved the application of statistical methods. The interpretation called for a critical examination of the results in the light of limitation of the study and the results of previous research in the field.

Some of the objectives are covered to find out the level of significance of University of Lucknow and its associated college teachers' attitude towards conservatism and radicalism in there areas of life, namely—personal area, social area and economic area of Professors, Readers and Lecturers.

Other objectives were concerned with finding out the difference between male and female teachers' attitude towards conservatism and radicalism with respect of age, educational qualification, rank, family setting, economic income, religion and cast. To analyze the data following statistics were required-

Mean

The mean of a distribution is commonly understood as the arithmetic average. The term grade-point average familiar to students in a mean value: it is computed by dividing the some of all the scores by the number of scores.

Standard Deviation

The standard deviation concept was introduced by Karl Pearson in 1893. It is by far the most important and widely used measure of studying dispersion. Its significance lies in the fact that it is free from those defects from which the earlier methods suffer and satisfies most of the properties of a good measure of dispersion. Standard deviation is also known as root mean squared deviations from the arithmetic mean. Standard deviation is denoted by the small Greek letter, σ (read as sigma).

The standard deviation measures the absolute dispersion or variability of a distribution, the greater the amount of dispersion or variability the greater the deviation for the greater will be the magnitude of the deviations of the values from their mean. A small standard deviation means a high degree of uniformity of the observations as well as homogeneity of a series, a large standard deviation means just the opposite. Thus few have two or more comparable series with identical or nearly identical means, it is the distribution with the smallest standard deviation that has the most representative mean. Hence standard deviation is extremely useful in judging the representativeness of the mean.

For calculating standard deviation in discrete series any of the following methods may be applied:

(1) Actual mean method.

(2) Assumed mean method.

(3) Step deviation method.

In the present study the investigator had applied step deviation method. When this method is used we take a common factor from the given data. The formula for computing standard deviation is

$$\sigma = \sqrt{\frac{fd'^2}{n} - \frac{fd'}{n}} \times c$$

(Gupta S.P, P. E 8-18)

TESTING STATISTICAL SIGNIFICANCE

The test of the significance of the difference between two means is known as a "t test". It involves the computation of the ratio between experimental variance (observed difference between two sample means) and error (variance the sampling error factor).

THE SIGNIFICANCE OF THE MEAN

(1) The Standard Error of the Mean (^{s}M) in Large Samples

The need for a standard error for a sample mean can best be understood when we have examined the factors upon which the stability of this statistic depends. The formula for the standard error for the mean is —

$$\text{SEM or } {}^{s}M = \frac{\sigma}{\sqrt{n}}$$

Where

s =the standard deviation of the population

n= the number of case in the sample

(2) The Standard Error of the Mean in Small Samples-

Whenever n is less than about 30 the formula for the ^{s}M is

$$SM = \frac{s}{\sqrt{n}}$$

in which, s= SM = $\sqrt{\frac{X^2}{n-1}}$ and n is the size of the sample.

(Garrett, Page 191)

The SE of the Difference between two independent means

To discover whether two groups differ sufficiently in mean performance to enable us to say with confidence that there is a difference between the means of the population from which the sample were drawn, we need to know the standard error of the difference between the two sample mean. Two situations arise with respect to differences between means: (1) those in which the means are uncorrelated, and (2) those in which the means are correlated.

1) *The standard SE of difference ('D) when means are uncorrelated and Samples are Large-*

The formula for the SE of the difference between uncorrelated or independent mean is-

$$^sD = {}^s(M_1 - M_2) = \overline{\sigma^2 M_1 + \sigma^2 M_2}$$

$$^sD = \sqrt{\frac{\sigma^2 1}{N_1} + \frac{\sigma^2 2}{N_2}}$$

in which,

$^sM_1$= the SE of the mean of the first sample

$^sM_2$= the SE of the mean of the second sample

^sD= the SE of the difference between the two sample means

N_1 and N_2 = sizes of the two samples.

A critical ratio or CR found by dividing the difference between the samples mean by its standard error ($CR=D/{}^sD$)[1]. This operation reduces the obtained difference to a 0 score and enable us to measure it off along the base line of the sampling distribution of differences.

2) *The SE of the difference between M's in small independent Samples-*

When the N's of two independent samples are small (less than 30) the SE of the difference between two means should depend upon SD's computed by the formula $S = \sqrt{\frac{X^2}{n-1}}$ and the degrees of freedom in the two groups must be taken into account.

The statistical significance of the difference between means, two additional concepts are also important. These are-

1) The null hypothesis
2) The level of significance

The Null Hypothesis (H_0)-

A null hypothesis states that there is no significant differences or relationships between two or more parameters. It concerns a judgement as to whether apparent differences or relationships or whether they merely result from sampling error. The experiments formulate for statistical purpose a null hypothesis, a no difference or relationship hypothesis. Although a null hypothesis is needed for statistical purposes, most actual hypothesis is needed for statistical purposes, most actual hypothesis are alternatives to the null, that is, hypothesis that purpose that differences will exist.

The use of the null hypothesis is not restricted to experimental studies. It may be used when inferring generalizations about populations from sample data in descriptive studies.

If the difference between these was not great enough to reject the null hypothesis, the researcher fails to reject it. He or she concludes that there was no significant difference and that chance or sampling error probably accounted for any observed difference.

The Level of Significance

Whether a difference is to be taken as statistically significant or not depends upon the probability that the given difference could have arisen "by chance". It also depends upon the purposes of the experiment. Usually, a difference is "significant" when the gap between two sample means point to or signifies a real difference between the parameters of the populations from which our samples were drawn.

Experimenters and research workers have for convenience chosen several arbitrary standards—called levels of significance—of which the 0.05 (1,96), 0.01 (2.58) levels are most often used. The confidence with which an experiments rejects—or retains-the null hypothesis upon the level significance adopted. When a CR is 1.96 or more we may reject a null hypothesis at the 0.05 level of significance. If the CR is 2.58 or higher, we reject the null hypothesis at the 0.01 level, on the grounds that not more than once in hundred trial would a difference or size arise if the true difference were zero.

REFERENCE

1. CR really equals (M1-M2)/°D the difference (D) between the two sample means is taken from 0.00 in terms of D.

Chapter 5
Bio Data

The role of the teachers in a society is well known to all. Nation's well being depends on the care for the teachers. Kothari Commission has very aptly observed that, the future of the nation is shaped in the class rooms. According to Gibran[1], "the teacher works in the shadow of the temple among his followers, gives not only of his wisdom but weather of his faith and his lovingness." The university is one of the organizations of conserving, transmitting and creating Knowledge College Teaching in India is an occupation that has lost a good deal of its social prestige and economic rewards in the post, independence period.[2]

The loss in prestige of teachers, however is not only due to the salary structure but there are also other causes such as lack of autonomy and control over their conditions of work, virtual lack of authority and poor conditions and environment (A.P. Bali). The features present in the ancient system of education are unfortunately conspicuous by there absence in the present days. We no longer find the ancient glory of the teacher. The situation reflects the teachers' present status. The pupil-teacher relationship at present is quite different from what prevailed in those days.

Prof. S.N. Mukherji[3] remarks that, " *the present day teacher has no status, no stability of service and consequently no peace of mind"*. All the tributes paid to the profession like nation building, "*man making*", "*noble*" and "*sacred*" are only high sounding empty words.

Teachers like other members in the society, though the influence of their culture and references groups, norms learns to believe in the centrality of work roles in life. They learn to value work because of part parental, school and religious socialization. They maintain their normative beliefs because of present socialization through reference group support and favourable environmental conditions. The reason for exploring the nature of such characteristics as age, marital status, religion and caste, educational qualification, income, professional rank is to put the teaching professionals, within the framework of their social background to enable to understand the correlates of the professional attitude and behaviour of teachers.

SOCIAL BACKGROUND

It is a well known fact that an individual's social background plays a vital role in the formation of the attitudes and values. To understand clearly the diversity of the respondents, it is necessary to study their sex, age, caste, marital status, education, family, number of children, occupation etc. for their social background.

Karl Manheim (1936) rightly said, "the opinions statements, proportions and system of ideas are not taken at their face value but are interpreted in the light of the life situation of the one who expressed them."[4] It is because of this reason that sociologists are interested in the study of the social background of their subjects.

SEX

Women are half the human race, yet the division of labour between the sexes was humankind's first act of social domination, and the inequality it produced has endured throughout all history and has been reproduced in all human societies. Sexual inequality is deeply rooted in the myths and values of culture, in the social roles accorded each sex and in the long-lasting conception of what is masculine and what is feminine.

Some feminists and some social scientists find it useful to consider that women are minority, like blacks and Hispanics. Yet there is a difference, too, because of both their numbers and their roles. It is not only that women are not numerical minority; neither are they a suppressed majority held in their "place" by a small ruling elite.

More to the point men and women live in intimacy and bondage to one another through the act of sexual reproduction and the expression of sexuality. Also by birth and marriage, women share with men their class and ethnic status.

The feminist demand for equality implies consequences far deeper than that of equal access to the position of the class structure.

Every effort to explain sexual inequality is in some way or other based on a conception of differences, it is usually claimed make it "natural" that men should dominate.

But such claims often confuse what it is that women and men derive from nature and what they acquire culture. They confuse, that is, the biology of sex with the cultural attributes of gender.

The Biological Difference

If one were to look for biological differences to explain male domination, what would one look for? It is women who bear children and nurse them and this is a primary biological difference between and women and men. Being children has conservancies for what women can and cannot do, at limited in their social and economic activity. But that is not reason for male domination.

The most obvious case for the biological superiority of males probably lies in the evidence of greater height and weight and in the musculature (the body's muscular system) which men possess. Men, in short, are physically stronger than women when strength is measured by muscle power.

But males are not stronger than females when strength is measured in ways. They start life with less capacity than women to survive physically. More of them are stillborn, and more of them die in the first of life; more males are born malformed, and more suffer injuries at birth. They are less resistant than females to diseases, and they can not bear pain as well. In short, if men are larger and stronger, women are more durable.

A review of a great range of research in human biology and in psychology provided very little evidence that these are fixed, determined behavioural propensities in either males or females.[5] It is not biology that creates such clear differences between how women and men act, and it is not biology that requires that males be dominant over females. Instead, the available evidence from primate studies, from studies of human infants, and from the studies of adult hormones shows "that biology constrains but does not determine the behaviour of the sexes and that differences between are physical constitutions and our patterns of social life.[6]

Nature and culture interact is most complex ways to shape men and women into the human beings they actually are.

The Cultural Difference

Social scientists have long insisted that it is culture not biology, which primarily determines human personality and the organization of social roles, human beings become persons and develop a self through socialization. Until very recently, instead, social scientists used a biosocial explanation of the differences between the sexes. They believed that social roles appropriate to each sex were determined by two basic biological facts that men are physically stronger than women and that also they felt accounts for the existence of "masculine" and "feminine" personalities appropriate to these roles.

The idea went like this: men being stronger, undertook the more strenuous task like hunting and fighting enemies, while women, limited by child-bearing and child care, performed simpler tasks nearer the home. Anthropologists, in fact, have often made of great deal out of this separation of sexual task in early humans and credited the male speciality of hunting with being a significant turning point in human evolution, one from which "our intellect, interests, emotions, and basic social life" are divided as "evolutionary products."[7]

Sociologists in turn have updated this idea for a time when men no longer hunt for a living. Men have been defined as task specialists, who organize practical activities and provide for the material needs of the family, while women are seen as socioemotional specialists who provide warmth, love and emotional support. [8] Two specialized roles—'One instrumental, the other expressive—are thus presumed to be linked to the biological characteristics of the sexes. It would be apparent to any woman that this is a singularly male view. These are obviously numerous task specialities associated with the caring for children, preparing food, and maintaining a house. House work may be unpaid labour, but it is a set of tasks which require work and organization.

Maccoby and Jacklin's thorough analysis of the research on sex differences led them to conclude that there is far less difference between the sexes in social behaviour, intellectual abilities, and motivations than has been assumed. Only four differences, they are really well established by research; girls have greater verbal ability; boys possess more mathematical skill are superior in visual-spatial ability and are more aggressive.[9]

Women's power and status are greater in those societies in which they have a role outside the family—particularly an economic role[10] when the control money and goods and dominate the market, as females traders in many societies do, they have real if not dominant power while most women in preindustrial societies contributed on whether or not they controlled what they produced. That is why women who were traders exercised more power than women who were tillers of the soil.

The Feminist Movement: Toward Sexual Equality

When women's struggle for equality took a more militant form and something called "women's liberation" came upon the scene, most men (and probably most women, too) thought that such a revolt of women against their traditional sex role was something new in American history. But was not.

The struggle for women's rights in fact has deep roots. In Italy, for example where women attended universities in the fourteenth and fifteenth centuries, they demanded equality of rights. But the women in that period were not in a position to foment rebellion. The feminist spirit was still largely restricted to a small group of women who were educated and middle or upper class.

The period of the 1840's was one of ferment and change in a still young and developmeng united status. Utopian communities thrived, religious rivivals swept the country, and a movement for the abolition of slavery began. A small but active number of middle-class women played a major role in these reform's participation in the antislavery struggle led to a national meeting in Seneca Falls, New York in 1848, where 300 women and men issued a Declaration of sentiments, a plea for ending the inequality of women in all aspect of life. Feminist theory is that part of the new Scholarship on women that impticitly or formally presents a generalized, wide-ranging system of ideas about the basic features of social life and of human experience as these can be understood from a women-centered in three ways. First its major "object" for investigation, the starting point of women in society. Second, it treats women as the central "Subjects" in the investigative process; that is it seeks to see the world from the distinctive vantage point of women in that social world. Third feminist theory is critical and activist on behalf of women, seeking to produce a better world for women—and thus, it argues, for humankind.

Although a focus on gender differences is a minority position in contemporary feminism some influential contributions to modern feminist theory do take this approach (Berni Kow, 1980, Gilligan, 1982, Kesler and McKenna, 1978; J. Miller, 1976; Ruddick, 1980, Snitow, 1979). The central theme in the contemporary literature on gender difference is that women's inner psychic life is, in its overall configuration, different from that of men. In their basic values and interests (Ruddick, 1980) their mode of making value judgements (Gilligan, 1982), their construction of achievement motives (Kaufman and Richardson, 1982), their literacy creativity (Gilbert and Gub ar, 1979) their sexual fantesies (Hite, 1976; Radway, 1984; Snitow et al., 1983) their sense of identity (Laws and Schwartz, 1977), and their general procession of consciousness and selfhood (Kasper, 1986, J. Miller, 1976), women bring a different vision and a different voice to the construction of social reality. A second theme is that the overall configuration of women's relationships and life experiences is distinctive.

But beyond these matters lies an even more basic one. Women have discovered that liberation from confinenment to domestic roles has not, however, freed them from the burdens of housework and child care. Even as they work full-time, they remain almost full time mothers and wives.

Yet as far back as 1970 a majority of women has expressed the desire that men share their domestic. Sociologist John Huber made the point sharply,"that women can bear children is to date, a fact of nature, but that women are assigned the responsibility of rearing children is a man-made fact subject to change. Even though no man has a womb, it is now technologically possible for men to share equally is the important and delicate task of socializing the next generation".[10] It is the responsibility for child care that will bear ultimately decisive for women's fate as the second sex or as the equal of man.

Radical Feminism

Central to radical feminism is an intense positive valuation of women and, as part of this, deep grief and rage over their oppression.[11] Radical Feminists affirm women's special worth in defiance of a universal system that devalues her, they rage at women's oppression by presenting a detailed and shocking catalogue of the offences committed against her worldwide. In this passionate mixture of love and rage, radical feminists resemble the more militant mode of racial and ethnic groups, the "black is beautiful" claims of black Americans or the detailed "witnessing" of oppression by Jews. As we explore radical feminist's appeal on behalf of women, we also can see quite clearly their position on Social Organization, greater oppression, and strategies for change.

Radical feminist see all society as characterized by oppression. Every institution is a system by which some people dominate others, and in society's most basic structures, in the associated patterns between broad groups or categories of people, one perceives a continuous pattern of domination and submission—between classes; castes; racial ethnic and religions groups; age and gender categories of all these systems of domination and subordination, the most fundamental structure of oppression is gender the system of patriarchy. Not only was patriarchy, as Engels described. Through participation in patriarchy men learn how to hold other human beings in contempt to see them as non-human, and to control them. Patriarchy to radical to radical feminists, is the least noticed and yet the most significant structure of social inequality.

Central of this analysis is the image of patriarchy as violence practised by men and male-dominated organizations against women. Violence may not always take the form of overt physical cruelty. It can be hidden in more complex practices of exploitation and control in standards of fashion and beauty; in tyrannical ideals of motherhood, monogram, chastity and hetero-sexuality; in the sexual harassment in the work place; in the practices of gynaecology, obstetrics, and psychotherapy; in unpaid household drudgery and underpaid wage work. Violence exists whenever one group controls in its own interests the life chances, environments, actions, and perceptions of another group, as men do women.

But the theme of violence as overt physical cruelty lies at the heart of radical feminism linking of patriarchy to violence: rape, sexual abuse, sexual slavery in enforced prostitution, spouse abuse, incest, sexual molestation of children, hysterectomies and other excessively radical forms of surgery and the explicit sadism in pornography are all linked to the historic and cross-cultural practices of witch burning, the stoning to death of adulteresses, the persuasion of icsbians, female infanticide, Chinese foot-binding, the forced suicides of Hindu widows, and the savage practice of clitoretomy. Thought the radial lens, we are given an image of women mutilated and bleeding as the visual representation of what patriarchy does.

Patriarchy exists as a near-universal social form ultimately because men can muster the most basic power resource, physical force, to establish control. Once patriarchy place, the other power resource–economic, ideological, legal, and emotional—also can be marshalled to sustain it. But physical violence always remains its last line of defence, and in both interpersonal and intergroup relations that violence repeatedly is used to protect patriarchy from women's individual and collective resistance.

Men create and maintain patriarchy not only because they have the resource to do so but because they have real interests in making women serve as compliant tools. Women are, for one thing, a uniquely effective means of satisfying male sexual desire. Their bodies are, further, essential to the production of children, who satisfy both practical and as psychoanalysts have shown, neurotic needs for men. Women are a useful labour force, as the Marxians have noted. They also can be ornamental signs of male, they are pleasant partners, sources of emotional support, and useful foils who reinforce, over and over again, the males' senses of their own central social significance. These useful functions mean that men everywhere seek to keep women compliant. But differing social circumstances give different rank orders to these functions and therefore lead to cross-cultural variations in the pattering of patriarchy. Radical feminists, unlike psychoanalytical feminists, give us both an explanation of universal gender oppression and a model for understanding cross-cultural variations in this oppression.

How is patriarchy to be defeated? Radical should that his defeat must begin with basic reworking of women's consciousness so that each woman recognizes her own and strength; rejects patriarchal pressures to see herself as weak, depender and second-class; and works in unity with other women, regardless of differences among them, to establish a broad-based sisterhood of trust, support, appreciation, and mutual defence. With this sisterhood in place, two strategies suggest themselves a critical confrontation with any facet of patriarchal domination whenever it is encountered; and a degree of separatism as women withdraw into women-run business, households, communities, centres of artistic creativity, and love relationships.

How does one evaluate radial feminism? Emotionally each of us will respond to it in light of our own degree of personal radicalism, some seeing it as excessively critical and others as entirely convincing. But in attempting a theoretical evaluation, one should note that radical feminism incorporates arguments made by both Marxian and psychoanalytical feminists about the reasons for women's subordination and yet moves beyond those theories. It is the broadest of the variants of feminism that we have thus for encountered. Radical feminists, more ever, have done significant research to support their thesis that patriarchy ultimately rests on the practice of violence against women (Barry, 1979; Bunch, 1987; Dworkin, 1987; 1989; Frye, 1983; Griffin, 1978, 1981; Millet, 1970; Rich, 1976, 1980).

In India traditional sex roles socialization indicates the belief that men are ones who should work build careers for themselves and provide economic support for the family and the families on the other side should except the roles of housewife. Such socialization has led to expectations that men as a group of might show more work involvement than women who would find role conflict between family rule and work roles. However, the traditional socialization forms are undergoing change, and to extent to which sex as variable will continue to carry with aspects of professional work is an important question with regard to the teaching profession which at least in the University of Lucknow and its associated degree colleges employees. Such a sufficient number of female Lecturers and Readers. In the samples of 388 teachers (160 from Lucknow University and 180 from associated degree colleges) there were 41% female teachers on three ranks—Lecturers, Readers and Professors. 59% male teachers were Lecturers, Readers and Professors from the university level and degree college level (Table 5.1).

Table 5.1
Distribution of Male and Female Teachers from Lucknow University and its associated Degree Colleges

	University Level		*College Level*			*Total*	*%*
M/F		*Number*	*%*	*M/F*	*Number*	*%*	
Male	47	64.6	Male	80	53.4	177	59
Female	53	35.4	Female	70	46.6	123	41
Total	150			150		300	

AGE

Age is related to the amount of experience members of the profession have, had, as well as the time spent on other jobs. For the respondents as a who, a very large proportion (100%) of the teaching staff joined the teaching profession as Lecturers and continued to be in the same position. Table 5.2 reveals that nearly three fourths (68.67%) of the teaching staff in the university and its associated degree college were between 20 to 45 years. The mean age of the teachers were found as 36.1.

Table 5.2
Age distribution of Lucknow University and its associated Degree College Teachers

Age-Group	*University Level* Teachers (M/F)	*%*	*College Level* Teachers (M/F)	*%*	*Total*	*%*
20-25	5	3.33	7	11.67	12	4.00
25-30	9	6.00	23	15.33	32	10.60
30-35	18	12.00	23	15.33	41	13.67
35-40	23	15.30	33	22.00	56	18.66
40-45	28	18.60	31	20.67	59	19.66
45-50	24	16.00	28	18.67	52	17.33
50-55	43	28.60	5	3.33	48	16.00
Total	150		150		300	

RELIGION AND CASTE

Sociologists find religion a relevant field in inquiry because religion is a social phenomenon. Moreover, a sociologist concentrates on issues and questins which are not generally considered by theologians and philosophers. The sociologist of religion focuses on the links between religion and other social phenomena such as politics, economics, science and technology. The sociologist of religion is not bound in his/her professional writing to accept prescriptions of a particular religion. A recent book on religion by Lawson and MacCauley (1990:v) is dedicated to those who taught that "... religion need not be a force to be feared nor a dogma to be embraced, but simply a way of life.[12]

Every society has religious beliefs, rites and organisations. Religion very often affects our understanding of every life. The way in which we relate to each other is very often influenced by our religious beliefs. Religion is also related to politics, and to economic activities like production, distribution and consumption. Religion can unite human beings together, but also sow hatred among them. Religion may produce differing impacts in different places. At one end of the globe, it serves to justify oppression and unequal distribution of resources. The same religion, you may find, serve as a reason to resist and struggle against oppression at the other end of the globe. If religious beliefs are the same then how do we explain why people react differently in different parts of the world? All religions teach love and universal brotherhood. Even then, why do people 'fight' amongst themselves and 'die' in the name of religion? It is precisely these sets questions, and the like which a sociologist studies. In a book on *Religion. Society and the Individual,* Yinger (1957:xu) wrote that religion is a social pehnomenon, because it is "woven into the fabric of social life."

Both religion and society have positive as well as negative effects on each other. Apart from this, sociologists also study the relationship between religion and various other social institutions like education, government and economy. They try to study the separate meaning of religion for various groups and levels in a society.

A sociologist may be a believer, and need not necessarily study religion. But if one is interested in the mutual interaction between religio and society, there are a number of issues one can investigate, for example, rituals, sects, or different aspects of a religion or a whole of religion as it operates in different settings. In other words, a sociologist has a vast domain from which to choose the particular area of study. Whether god exists or not is not a question a sociologist is interested in. Sociology of religion cannot prove or disprove the existence of god, or judge whether a set of values are right or wrong. Sociology of religion is not an agenda of socio-religious reform.

Religion, first and formost, involves a group of people. Religion is a shared system of beliefs and practices. Every religion emphasises the need for collective worship. Festivals and rituals are occasions which bring people together. M.N. Srinivas[13] (1978 : 202) in his study of Coorg villages observes that the festivals of village deities include of village-dance, collective hunt and a dinner for entire village. The collective dinner, in which the entire village participates, is called 'urorome' (village-harmony). Durkheim[14] (1912), a pioneering sociologist, equates god with society, so much so that, when you worship God you are worshipping your own society. According to Durkheim God is a human creation and a social creation at that. God is, in fact, born in the collective experience ("effervscence") of coming together, leading to rituals.

Religious belief is a system of knowledge about the divine and its relationship with the human. It is simply not enough to believe in the existence of a supernatural force.

The knowledge of its existence must be explained to people and to generations to come. Belief serves this purpose of revealing the existence of the supernatural or divine or the sacred. Belief explains the nature of the divine, the deeds, actions or words of the divine and prescribes ways in which human beings can communicate with the divine.

Religion has played a very important role in shaping the life, conduct and various activities of human beings. Generally everyone in the world follows one or the other religion or faith. However, it is not easy to precisely define religion. Some people who have a scientific bent of mind believe that religion did not possess the broad outlook in their early days which they possess today. Science has considerably helped in removing superstitions and blind following. It has broken many conservative traditions. The science however never says that one should not follow a religion. Religion prescribes human values, Ideals, cultured traditions, moral conduct for the human society.

India is a multi-religious society. The two major communities are Hindus and Muslims, the former are however, in a majority. As such most teacher positions are in the hand of Hindus though Muslims who constitute about one eighths of 12% of India's population of 87 crores, also have their share of these positions in the wider society. Chanchal Sarkar[15] observes, "*Caste and community still remains troublesome, inhibiting factors in the University.*" The 1969, Gajendragadkar Commission Report on the Banaras Hindu University also confirms and highlights the role of casts and religion in university politics. Needless to say that Lucknow University is no exception to the intrusion of castes and religion in University administration and teachers selection and politics.

Now caste-wise most teachers position are held by upper caste Hindus. Chiefly the Brahmins (like traditional Indian

Social System), and this is also true of teachers profession, as shown in Table 5.3.

Table 5.3

Religion and Caste composition of Lucknow University and its associated degree college teachers

Religion & Caste	*University Level Teachers (M/F)*	*%*	*College Level Teachers (M/F)*	*%*	*Total*	*%*
1. Hindu	(100)	(66.67)	(47)	(31.33)	(147)	(48.66)
(i) Brahman	50	33.33	15	10.00	65	21.66
(ii) Chatriya	25	16.6	15	10.00	40	13.33
(iii) Vaishya	21	13.3	10	6.66	31	10.00
(iv) Shudra & Backward	4	2.6	7	4.66	11	3.66
1. Muslim	(37)	(24)	(81)	(54)	(118)	(39)
(A) Sunni	[22]	[14.66]	[38]	[25.33]	[60]	[20]
(i) Syed	13	8.66	20	13.33	33	11
(ii) Khan	6	4	14	9.33	20	6.66
(iii) Ansari	3	2	4	2.6	7	2.33
(B) Shia	[15]	[9.33]	[43]	[28.66]	[58]	[19]
(i) Syed	8	5.33	30	20	38	12.66
(ii) Shiekh & Mughal	7	2.66	13	8.66	20	5.66
(iii) Pathan	0	0	0	0	0	0
3. Christian	(13)	(8.66)	(22)	(14.66)	(35)	(11.66)
(i) Catholic	5	3.33	11	7.33	16	5.33
(ii) Protestant	8	5.33	11	7.33	19	6.33

The religious composition of university and its associated degree college teachers shows (Table 5.3) that the overwhelming majority of teachers were Hindus (48.66%) and Muslims (39%). It is also noteworthy that there were 11% teachers belonging to the Christian faith (Catholic and Protestant).

Now caste-wise most teachers positions in university and colleges are held by upper caste Hindu (21.66%) and Muslim (23.66%), chiefly the Brahmins and Muslim Syed.

In fact it is noteworthy that the caste composition of teachers completely confirmed to the traditional hierarchical ordering of castes, in which Brahmins are at the top, followed by Kshatriyas and Vaishays in that order. The Shudra or backward Class of Shudra teachers were 3.6% (as shown in the Table 5.3).

The percentage of Muslim backwards (Ansari) were 2.33% (as shown in Table 5.3). It may however be pointed out that what is most frequently described and analyzed as caste conflict is in rarity class conflict in that the upper caste are also the owing classes and that the lower or backward castes belonged to the have not, non-owing, exploited classes.

Table 5.4
Distribution of University and its Associated Degree College teachers on the basis of their ranks

Rank	*University Level* Teachers (M/F)	%	*College Level* Teachers (M/F)	%	*Total*	%
(i) Professors	50	33.33	0	0	50	16.66
(ii) Readers	50	33.33	80	26.66	130	43.33
(iii) Lecturers	(50)	(33.33)	(70)	(23.33)	(120)	(40.00)
(A) Temporary	7	4.6	10	3.33	17	5.66
(B) Permanent	43	28	60	20	103	34.33

RANK OF TEACHERS

The data was collected on three ranks—Lecturers, Readers and Professors from university level and its associated degree college level. Table 5.4 shows that rank wise 16.66% teachers were Professors, 43.33% were Readers and 40% were Lecturers, in which 5.66% were temporary Lecturers and 34.33% teachers were permanent Lecturers at both levels.

Table 5.4 reveals that Professors are in a few numbers in comparison of Readers and Lecturers, there were only 1% female professors in the University of Lucknow.

FAMILY STRUCTURE

Family is one of the permanent social institution, which is find in one form or another, in almost all societies of the world. There are a large number of Scholars who have discussed the importance of family institutions for its members.[16]

One of the most classical and functional explanations of family was given by MacIver and Page.[17] They say the family is a group defined by a sex relationship sufficiently precise and ending to provide for the procreation and up bringing of children. The social institution of family is built around the needs of human beings to regularise sexual behaviour and protect the young ones. It is the backbone of our social structure and reveals a remarkable continuity through ages. The family, as we see it today, is a durable association of husband with or without children. The Indian family may mean a much larger one including grand parents, relatives in, laws and grandchildren, all comprising a unit, which is called household. Some of the traditional family functions in India include financial help to relatives in times of need, providing facilities for education, religious guidance, personal security, affection and social exchange to its members. As an institution, the family has not perished since its basis is the fundamental need of human beings to be together.

According to Cooley, the sociologist, and Freud, the psychoanalyst, the most important or analysts treats class as the basic personality-shaping group force, saying that the family is but a part of the super structure and is therefore itself shaped (In terms of structure and values) by the economic systems. Thus, the family can not be viewed in isolation from a society's economic framework, the family, in other words, is a dependent variable.

The fact, however remains that the family has became a major conception tool sociological research and analysis.

Family is one of the primary look for individual. Besides being necessary for the human beings it is primary center for them to learn many things. Physical and mental bent of an individual somewhat depends on family. Formation of personality and process of socialization start in family. Very tender feeling of human beings take shape in the family even choice of small nuclear family finds its instinct in the atmosphere in the family. The future of joint families are dark (Table-5.5).

Table 5.5
Family Structure of University and its Associated Degree College Teachers

Structures	*University Level Teachers (M/F)*	*%*	*College Level Teachers (M/F)*	*%*	*Total*	*%*
Joint Family	19	12.6	38	25.4	25.7	19.00
Nuclear Family	131	87.4	112	74.6	2.43	81.00
Total	150	100	150	100	300	100

Data collected under Table 5.5 reveals that, most of the teachers belong to nuclear families, as the joint family having disorganized, number of nuclear families is increased. Since the nuclear families are greater in number, 81% teachers belong to the nuclear families. The percentage of teachers belonging to the joint families was only 19 per cent.

MARITAL STATUS

The path to marriage is linked with a variety of impediments, requirements, preliminaries, and ceremonials which would be downright discouraging—were not the objective so compelling. Rare is the society which simply allows a couple quietly to pair off the start playing house. Marriage is too important for such casual arrangements. Marriage is the *approved social pattern whereby two or more persons establish a family.* It involves not only the conceiving and rearing of children (who are sometimes conceived as an institutionalized preliminary to marriage), but also a host of other obligations and privileges affecting a good many people. Every society has, therefore, developed a pattern for guiding these marriages.

In this matter a guidance our enthnocentrism is likely to be evident. To us it is monstrous that parents should arrange and compel the marriage of two persons who may never even have met! How do they know whether they will love each other? Why are not their wishes consulted? Our creation illustrates the usual error of ethnocentrism—assuming that people of another culture will think and feel if transplanted into their situation. It overlooks the fact that most people wish and feel only what their culture trains them to wish and feel. We think of marriage as a romantic adventure with a person we have come to love. The girl in classical China, about to enter in arranged marriage with a stranger, eagerly anticipated her marriage as a desirable status and a comfortable companionship with a man she would come to love, because he had been wisely chosen by her parents. Each society viewed the other with an ethnocentric pity; we pitied their young people for their lack of freedom; they pitied our young people for their lack of parental assistance. In neither case did the young people themselves feel any need for pity. Today, of course, the Chinese family is changing rapidly and painfully under the new Peoples' Republic (Levy, 1949; Chandrasekhar, 1959; Yang, 1959; Huang, 1961).

Endogamy and exogamy: Every society limits choice in marriage by requiring that one choose a mate outside his own group. This is called exogamy. In our society the prohibition applies only to close blood relatives; one may not marry his sister, first cousin, and certain other close relatives. Many societies extended the circle of prohibited kin to forbid marriage within the clan, the village, or sometimes even the tribe.

Most societies also require that mates be chosen within some specified group. This is called *endogamy*. Clan, village, and tribal endogamy are quite common among primitive societies.

Every society practices both exogamy and endogamy, as it specifies the limits of group closeness (exogamy) and the limits of group distance (endogamy) within which mates must be found. Sometimes between these two limits there is little room for hunting! The Aranda of Central Australia have a complicated marital pattern known to anthropologists as an "eight-class system with exogamy and indirect patrilineal descent." To skip the detailed explanations, this means that a man can marry only a woman from a particular group within the proper subsection of the opposite half of his tribe (Murdock, 1936, pp. 27-30). In a number of societies, a formula such as this makes an actual choice unnecessary, for only one girl may be in the permissible category for a boy to marry. If there is none at all, then the couple who are supposed to become his parents-in-law normally adopt a marriageable girl from another family with a surplus. After all, an institution is a structure for meeting human needs, and it usually does so in one fashion or another.

Marital Choice : The process of arranging a marriage shows a fascinating range of possibilities. As shown above, some societies follow a formula whereby the children of certain socially designated kinsmen marry each other, so that the individual choices may be unnecessary. Where actual choices are necessary they may be made in many ways. The couple can do their own choosing sometimes with parental guidance or parental veto. The parents can arrange the marriage with or without considering the couple's. A wife may be purchased, or perhaps a complicated series of gifts are exchanged between families. Wife capture is not unknown. All these patterns exist as the standard way of arranging marriages in some of the world's societies. All of them work within the society in which they exist—and are supported by the surrounding values and practices of the culture. Wife capture worked very well for the Tasmanians, who practised village exogamy and were not greatly concerned over the differences between one woman and all the others. For our society, it would be less practical.

Monogamy and Polygamy : To us, the only decent and civilized form of marriage is *monogamy*—one man to one woman (at a time). Yet a majority of the world's societies have practised *polygamy,* allowing a plurality of mates. There are three theoretical forms of polygamy. One is *group marriage,* in which several men and several women are all in a marriage relationship with one another. While this is an intriguing theoretical possibility, there is no authentic instance of it among human beings, with the possible exception, at one time, of the Marquesans. A very rare form is *polyandry,* where several husbands share a single wife. The Todas of Southern Indian provide one of our few examples. Here, as in most other cases, polyandry was fraternal, meaning that when a woman married a man, she automatically became wife to all of his brothers and they all lived together with little jealousy or discord. Toda polyandry becomes understandable when one learns that is accompanied female infanticide and a shortage of women (Murdock, 1936, pp. 120-121; Queen *et al.,* 1961, chap. 2). Only where some situation has created a shortage of women is polyandry likely to be found (Unni, 1958). But the scattered handful of societies which practice polyandry serve to show how a practice which seems to us to be contrary to human nature can still be the accepted and preferred pattern for people who are socialized to expect it. The usual form of polygamy is *polygyny*—a plurality of wives, not necessarily and generally acquired at different times during one's life.

It would be difficult to show that women have generally had a more satisfactory status in monogamous than in polygamous societies. Even in polygynous societies, most of the marriages are monogamous. It is generally only the more successful and powerful men who can afford or attract more than one wife. In many polygynous societies, the second wife fills the status function of the second Cadillac in our society. Far from feeling resentful, the first wife often urges her husband to take more wives, over whom she generally reigns as queen be.

Divorce : What is to be done when a married couple can't stand each other? Although most societies make some provision for divorce, some make it very difficult or perhaps give the privilege of divorce only to the men. Some make divorce very simple. Among the Hopi, divorce is rather rare but very uncomplicated. The husband merely packs up and leaves, or in his absence his wife tells him to get lost by piling his things outside the door.

The social and family structure of many societies makes divorce a fairly painless and harmless operation. Where there is no great emphasis upon romantic love and no intense individual love attachments, divorce entails no great heartbreak. Where the consanguine family surrounds the child with a protective clan of kin, and designates the mother's brother as the responsible male in a child's life, the loss of child's father is hardly noticed. The meaning of divorce depends upon how it relates to other aspects of the institution of the family. In our society, with its strong accent upon individual love attachments within an independent conjugal family unit, a divorce is likely to mean the collapse of the emotional world for both child and adult marriage is one of the basic social institutions which with its different forms and types is found in all societies of the world. Marital status has a significant bearing on social standing of a man or woman. It also leads to changes in attitudes, responsibilities and behaviour patterns.

In India, marriage is supposed to be a religious obligation. It confers a special states and provides due recognition to both men and women. It is therefore, necessary to have some knowledge about the marital status of our respondents in this study. If the marital couples want to enjoy activities that bring education and pleasurable opportunities to others, they are expected to be cooperative, methodical and painstaking. Happily married persons do not take offence easily for undue concern. Shown by others, not are they too much bothered about impressions they make on others.

In India Hindu and Muslim marriages are performed according to traditional ways of solemnizing them. Hindu marriage is performed according to Vedic rites and it is not a contract system. In Islamic tradition marriage has the character of a contract. Hence it allows divorce to both parties though on different conditions. The Indian Christians are governed by the Special Marriage Act of 1954. All the conditions laid down in the act for divorce are applicable to Christian couples. In addition divorce can be taken by mutual consent of spouses.

Due to influence of religion and caste marriage as an institution has specific image in Indian context. In broader context where we examine the concept of marriage, we find that due to heavy industrialization and modernization, the institution of marriage is losing its control and impact on human behaviour all over the world but in India social circumstances where marriage is an authorized are recognized institution and has no deep impact of social change, it is proper to make an investigation regarding teachers marital status.

Table 5.6

Marital Status of University and Degree College Teachers

Marital Status	*University Level Teachers (M/F)*	*%*	*College Level Teachers (M/F)*	*%*	*Total*	*%*
Married	115	76.6	85	36.77	200	66.7
Single	24	16.2	35	23.44	59	19.7
Divorcee	4	2.6	16	10.6	20	6.6
Widow	7	4.6	14	9.3	21	7.0

Present table reveals that the percentage of married teachers was greater 66.7% and unmarried teachers percentage was 19.7%. Divorcee teachers was 6.6% and widow were 7% in the whole sample.

CLASS BACKGROUND

Although the concept of social class has long been used by sociologists, some sociologists today feel that it is not a useful concept (Faris, 1954; Nisbet, 1959; Lasswell, 1965). They state that there are no definite boundaries or dividing lines for social classes, that persons placed in one class according to one measure belong in another class according to another, and that, consequently, the members of a "class" differ from the another too greatly for the concept of class be valid.

Is social class purely a matter of money? If so, the rich gambler would outrank the minister, nurse, or professor. While money is a factor, social class is not directly measured by one's bank account. *A social class is defined as a stratum of people of similar position in the social status continuum.* The social position of the janitor is not the same as that of the college president; a student will not greet them in exactly the same manner. We are deferential toward those whose social position we believe to be above ours; we are condescending to those whom we consider socially below us. These processes of snubbing and kowtowing, of trying to claw one's way in or shouldering out the person who doesn't "belong"—these provide the inexhaustible material for hundreds of novels, plays, and scripts every year.

The member of a social view one another as social equals, while holding themselves to be socially superior to some other groups and socially inferior to still others.

How many classes are there? This question is hard to answer. Classes are not sharply defined status groupings like the different ranks in an army. Social status varies along a continuum, a gradual slope from to bottom, rather than a series of steps. As "youth," "middle age," and "old age" are points along an age continuum, the several social classes may be viewed as points along a status continuum. Consequently, the number of social classes is not *fixed*, nor do any definite boundaries and sharp status intervals separate them. Instead, persons found at all status level from top to bottom, just as persons are found at all weights and heights, with no abrupt gaps in the series.

Such a series can be broken up into any convenient number of "classes." Clothing makers have found it practical to divide people into a dozen or more size classifications. Earlier students of social class broke up the status continuum into three classes—upper, middle, and lower. Later students found this division unsatisfactory for many communities, because it placed persons in the same class even when they were much too far apart to treat one another as equals. Later students have often used a sixfold classification by breaking each of these three classes into an upper and lower section. The top, or *upper-upper* class, is composed of the wealthy old families, who have long been socially prominent, and who have had money long enough for people to have forgotten when and how they got it. The *lower-uppers* may have as much money but have not had it as long, and their family has not long been socially prominent. The *upper-middle* class includes most of the successful business and professional men, generally of "good" family background and comfortable income. The *lower-middle* class takes in the clerks, other white-collar workers and semiprofessionals, and possibly some of the foremen and top craftsmen. The *upper-lower* class consists mainly of the steadily employed workers, and is after described as the "working class" by those who feel uncomfortable about applying the "lower" to honest workmen (Miller and Riessman, 1961).

All complex societies have some system of stratification which unequally ranks people. The extent and kind of inequality varies tremendously, but there are always some accepted standards by which men distinguish their peers from their inferiors. This is true in Communist countries which deplore class divisions and in capitalist countries which may justify them; it is true in both democrats and autocracies and in agricultural as well as industrial societies. The only possible exception is in the most primitive food-gathering societies where people lie by collecting roots and berries. Here there is little possibility of any division of labour and hence little possibility of rank which may lead to group differentiation.

Each social class is a system of behaviour, a set of values, and a way of life. While some overlapping and some exceptions occur, it remains true that the average middle-class child has a socialization vastly different from that of the average lower-class child.

Although social class includes many features besides occupation, it is fundamentally based on the division of labour. A complex society requires many workers with varying degree of skills and many coordinators with varying realms of authority. Prestige and power attach to the higher-ranked occupations and in turn enable the men in these occupations to confer advantages on their descendants. Thus a group of people arise whose hereditary privileges are greater than are those of people who have descended from less highly regarded ranks.

An agricultural society with only two or three categories of responsibility may have a completely rigid system of stratification in which the gulf between nobles and commoners is never bridged. An industrial society is apt to have a far greater variety of occupations with greater ease of movement from one level to another, but distinct levels still remain. Social class, then, grows out of the system of division of labour, and the ease of movement from one level to another depends upon the complexity and flexibility of the occupational structure of the society.

Such differences in class behaviour are found in virtually every activity of life—food habits, personal care, discipline and child care, reading tastes, conversational interests, vocabulary and diction, religious behaviour, sleeping arrangements, sex life.

DETERMINANTS OF SOCIAL CLASS

What places one in a particular social class? Is it birth, money, occupation, or what? The answer to each question is "yes," for all these attributes are involved.

(1) Wealth and Income

Money is necessary for upper-class position; yet one's class position is not directly proportional to his income a teacher has less status than college professor at half the income. To understand the place of money in class determination, we must remember that a *social class basically a way of life.* It takes a good deal of money to live as upper-class people live. Yet no amount of money will gain immediate upper-class status. Their children, however, have a better chance, and for their grandchildren, a secure upper-class status is practically assured. Money, *over a period of time,* usually gains upper-class status. People who get money begin to live like upper-class people. By the time their grandchildren mature, they are becoming "old family," while the grandchildren have fully absorbed upper-class behaviour. Thus the two requisites of upper-class status are fulfilled.

Money, then, is an important determinant of social class, partly because of the way of life it permits or enforces, and partly because of what it suggests about one's family background and way of life.

(2) Occupation

Occupation is another determinant of class status. As soon as man developed specialized kinds of work, he also got the idea that some kinds of work were more honourable than others. In a primitive society, the spear maker, the canoe builder, and the medicine man each holds a definite social status because of his work.

Just why one occupation should carry greater prestige than another is a question which has long fascinated social theorists. The high-prestige occupations generally receive the higher income; yet there are many exceptions. A popular nightclub singer may earn as much in a week as Supreme Court justice earns in a year.

The high ranking occupations generally require advanced education, but again the correlation is far from perfect. The importance of the work is an unsatisfactory test, for how can we sat that the work of the farm hand or policeman is less valuable to society that the work of the lawyer or corporation director? In fact, it has been suggested that the low-ranking garbage collector may be the most essential of all workers in an urban civilization! Obviously, the prestige ranking of occupations cannot be easily explained on a purely rational basis; yet it can hardly be an accident that all complex cultures have developed much the same hierarchy of occupational status. A survey of data from many countries by Inkeles (1960) finds that a particular occupation has about the same status rating in all urbanized, industrialized societies. Apparently the industrial system fosters certain attitudes, perceptions, and status relationship wherever it develops. And in all societies, industrial or preindustrial, we see that persons tend to be assigned a class status according to their occupation, and that people will find those occupations open to them which are appropriate to their present class status. Occupation is an exceedingly important aspect of social class because so many other facets of life are connected with occupation. If we know man's occupation, we can make some fairly accurate guesses about the amount and kind of education he has had, the standard of living he can afford, the kind of people he associates with, the hours he keeps, and the daily routines of his family life.

(3) Education

Social class and education interact in at least two ways. First, to get higher education one needs money plus motivation. Lack of money is less of a barrier that it used to be, now that scholarships and students loans are so widely available; yet relatively few students complete college without some financial aid from their families. Even if it is no more than free room, board, and laundry for all or part of the year, this is a considerable help. Upper-class youths already have money for the finest schools; they also have family, traditional and social encouragement. For the upper-class or upper-middle-class high-school youth, the question is, "What college are you going to?", lower, middle-class and perhaps upper-lower-class youths ask one another, "What will you do after graduation?"; lower-lower class youths are more likely to ask, "How soon can I quit school?" Second, one's amount and kind of education affects the class rank he will secure. Education is one of the main levers of the ambitious. Higher education brings not only occupational skills; it also brings changes in tastes, interests, goals, etiquette, speech—in one's total way of life. Level of education is probably the most important single clue to a man's social class.

Although a distinguished family background is a necessity for secure upper-class status, education may substitute for family background at the intermediate class levels. The middle classes are so large and move around so much that it is impossible to know the family background of each individual. Newcomers to a locality are likely to be accepted into whichever of the middle or lower classes their behaviour fits them. Education, occupation and expended income are three fairly visible clues, and with these are associated most of the other behaviour characteristics which make one "belong".

Size of each class

A measurement of classes is complicated by the fact that there are several criteria of membership in a given class and many families do not show all the characteristics of any one class level. For example, the "ideal type" lower-lower-class family would live in an urban slum or rural shack; one or more adult members would drink quite heavily, and the male family head would not be consistently in the household; the family would have little education or interest in education; and its low income would be derived partly from intermittent unskilled labour and partly from welfare sources. Probably comparatively few lower-lower-class families meet all of these conditions. While class differences are real, the boundaries and membership of each class cannot be clearly fixed.

The Significance of Social Classes

From before one is born until after he is dead, his opportunities and rewards are affected by his position. A study of Chicago death rates in 1940 found a life expectancy at birth of 61 years for the lower-class female and 70.3 years for the upper-class female, while for males the expectancies were 58.7 and 67.8 years, a difference of over 9 years for each sex. In the area of it is also true, that the school attended by the lower-class child has usually been one of the drab and dingly schools of the community. His teachers may be either dedicated mentors hopefully utilizing the latest educational methods or weary drudges who have long since given up in what seems a hopeless battle against ignorance and apathy.

Since social classes are subcultures, the personality development of the child is affected in many way (Davis and Havighurst, 1946; Sears et al., 1957; Havighurst and Davis, 1955). As has been already suggested, his goals, interests, and habits are affected by the kind of social world he lives in. His moral standards are equally class-typed. The lower-class family is less stable, more often broken by death or separation. It is larger in size, yet occupies smaller living quarters. At almost every point of contact between child and parent, there are class differences in socialization experience.

Middle-class child training encourages individual achievement and the urge to "succeed," encourages competition and rivalry while discouraging direct aggression, uses parental love systematically as a control device, avoids serve physical punishment, imposes numerous restrictions, and produces a good many anxieties and guilt feelings. Lower-class child training more rapidly pushes the child into adult roles, places less stress on individual achievement, accepts the idea that the child will probably retain the social status of its father, seldom uses parental love as a systematic reward, uses physical punishment readily, imposes fewer restrictions upon organic functions, literacy or school advancement.

As compared with lower-class personality, adult middle-class personality tends to be more ambitious, more competitive but less aggressive physically, more rigidly conformist to conventional mores, outwardly more poised and self assured, but possibly be set by greater inner guilts and self-doubts. Such differences are not predictably time for all members of either class, for there are many exceptions and much overlapping. But such differences are frequent enough to be socially significant. (Barber, 1957, chapter-12) The way people handle life situations varies with social class. Social class affects the way people deal with virtually every aspect of reality. As space forbids examining them all, let us describe just two areas of life in which class background appears to produce contradictory tendencies; political attitudes, in which the lower classes appear to be more liberal (some would say "radical"), and social attitudes, in which the lower classes appear to be more conservative. (The terms, "liberal" and "conservative" are here used to describe differing degrees of receptivity to social change).

Social Class and Political Attitudes

If social class influences the basic outlook of people, we should expect people to support the party and candidates closest to their class interests. Several surveys (Centres, 1949, chap. 5) seem to confirm this expectation in showing that the lower classes are more favourable toward government welfare benefits and services and government regulation of business than are the other classes.

Party alignment by social class is not perfect; some lower-class people vote Republican, and a few upper-class people vote Democratic. Class interest is not the only factor in voter behaviour, although it does appear to be the greatest factor. Whenever the political candidates are clearly identified with issues that appear to threaten or favour the welfare of a particular segment of the population, most members of that segment will vote accordingly.

In political attitudes and behaviour, then, social class appears to be the most important determinant. The loyal Republican or Democrat will defend his allegiance with a string of arguments without realizing that these particular arguments make sense to him largely because of his set of class interests, traditions, habits, and associations. Thus, on economic issues, the lower class tends to be politically liberal and the upper class politically conservative. Is this division true in other fields of interest besides economics?

Social Class and Social Attitudes

The lower-class tends to be liberal on economic questions but conservative in many other social attitudes. The lower class appear reluctant to accept new ideas and practices and is suspicious of the innovators. Changes in health practices, food usage, religious doctrines, family life, or educational procedures are likely to find their strongest opposition among lower-class groups. Their limited education, reading habits, and associations isolate the lower class from a knowledge of the reasons for these changes, and this ignorance, together with their class position, makes them suspicious of the middle and upper-class "experts" and "do-gooders" who promote the changes.

Many other examples of lower-class conservation could be cited. "Contemporary" design in art and home furnishings is first found in the shops catering to the wealthy and later is vulgarized for the lower-class tastes. The lower class is last to feel the trend toward the democratic family, permissive child-training practices, and birth control procedures (Bossard, 1954, chap. 15). It does not follow that *all* social changes filter downward from the top, but a pattern of lower-class conservatism does seem to apply to many activities and interests.

Social Class and Social Participation

Social class largely determines which parts of the culture one will experience—opera, country club, and cotillion, or jukebox, tavern, and brawl! This is illustrated by class differences in degree of social participation. In general, the lower the social class, the fewer are the associations and social relations of the individual.

The age of mass communications cuts across class lines, and while the lower classes read and travel less than classes, they spend more time with radio, television, and movies (Bogart, 1958, p. 91). This greater audiovisual exposure is still a selective process, since lower-class listeners shun "serious" programs and stick as far as possible to entertainment, which in turn is shaped along stereotypes already accepted in lower-class culture. Some of the patterns of behaviour related to social class are indicated in the following digest of class attitudes toward governmental, religious, and educational institutions. All these propositions are supported by research findings.

SUMMARY OF SOME CLASS ATTITUDES TOWARD SOCIAL INSTITUTIONS

Attitudes Toward Governmental Institutions

Upper class

Appreciate effect of government on own affairs; know leading official and are interested in politics. Majority will regard governmental regime as basic to their own security and will resist any type of drastic change. A minority will take their own security for granted and work energetically for an "efficient" or "humanitarian' regime.

Middle class

Conscious of duty to be "good citizens". Responsive to appeals for "clean" or "honest" government, but for the most part will resist major change.

Lower class

Many are completely indifferent to government since it seems remote and evidently has little effect on them. Some view it as the dispenser of petty favours such as minor jobs and possible payments for votes. A few may be consciously discontented with status and work for a revolutionary change that promises them greater benefits.

Attitudes Toward Religious Institution

Upper class

Often take positions of leadership in lay movement and like to be considered "patrons" of the church. Some are critical of church dogma, but interested in the aesthetic aspects of religion. Some feel above the need for religion and show little interest except when custom demands their attendance on special occasions.

Middle class

Apt to be responsive to appeals on a moral or intellectual basis. Somewhat uncertain about attitude toward traditional church dogmas. Highly critical of religious practices that seem to be excessively emotional.

Lower class

Responsive to emotional services with (among Protestants) little ritual. Protestant groups often accept highly puritanical dogma which is often evaded in practice. Readily accepts reports of modern miracles. Some feel that the church is an upper-class institution and are either indifferent or openly hostile. Many join "store-front" churches that stress emotional expression and informal association.

Attitudes Toward Economic Institution

Upper class

Take superior position and high standard to living for granted. Normally believe the traditional economic system is the best possible arrangement. Sometimes morally uneasy because of special privileges and seek to compensate by charity or civic service. Small minority may worry about "social injustice" and promote social reforms.

Middle class

Laud virtues of thrift, ambition, and "decent" living. Torn between desire to improve status by saving money and need to prove their importance by expensive living. Tend to accept prevailing system, but hope to rise within it.

Lower class

Usually take inferior position for granted. Have little real hope of improvement. Little chance for thrift, and occasional windfalls are used for immediate consumption. Some have acquired middle-class aspirations and seek rise in status through thrift and increased educational attainments. A few resent inferior position and hope for change through revolution and different type of economic structure.

Attitude Toward Educational Institution

Upper class

Many assume that their children will attend fashionable private schools and will make acceptable but not necessarily outstanding records. Education is regarded as a means of securing social acceptance and enriching cultural values rather than of preparation for earning a living. They support private school generously, but some oppose raising taxes for public education. Other send their children to public schools in fashionable neighbourhoods and to the major state universities. These parents are "patrons" of the schools and use their influence to increase community support of public education.

Middle class

Life adjustment, vocational preparation, and opportunity for meeting suitable marriage partners are major aspects sought in higher education. Parents are concerned about standards of public education, join parent-teacher associations, and generally support higher school taxes. Children are expected to have a good school record. Some view the degree or certificate as more important than the content of education. Such parents refuse to be involved in maintaining educational standards and may resist increases in taxes. These parents are anxious that students graduate but not greatly concerned about high marks.

Lower class

Many consider the school not very important, perhaps even a nuisance. Their children are not encouraged either to excel in studies or to remain in school. Increases in school taxes often receive the most opposition from this group. Some, especially among the upper-lowers, become "middle-class" converts who view the school as a channel of occupational mobility, and make great sacrifices to see that children have a chance for education.

Although class privileges and obligations differ, all classes make useful contributions to society, and all types of class environments produce individuals who are problems to themselves and to society. Whether a class system is the best means of assigning different social functions is probably a question of only academic interest, since all modern societies follow the system. Ethical interest focuses on two questions. First, should the privileges and responsibilities of different classes be modified in the direction of minimizing differences between them? And second, can, or should, we promote the opportunities for individuals to change their class levels? Most societies are now more or less seriously commited to a program of curtailing upper-class privileges and improving levels of living for the lower class.

Many social societists have specified the source of income as a criterion of class. The combination of what people do in the division of labour (occupation) or of what they own (property), as well as what they earn (income), can provice an adequate and revailing conception of stratification in economic terms. This concern constantly takes sociologists back to the writings of Karl Marx and Max Weber to understand what social class is.

Karl Marx's analysis of class begins with the recognition that the members of society are divided into economic strata, each stratum being made up of those who share a similar function in the organization of economic production. The division of labor, based upon the existing technology, creates a set of social relationships among people as workers. One of Marx's definitions of class says much of this.

"Insofar millioins of families live under economic conditions that separate their mode of life, their interests and their culture from those of other classes, and put them into hostile opposition to the latter, they form a class."[18]

This "hostile opposition" is for Marx, a necessary aspect of social class. In uniting to do, "common battle", against another class, a stratum of workers or peasants becomes a social class. A social class, in his conception, exists only in so far as an economic stratum is aware of and is prepared to struggle for its economic interests against another class: "the struggle of class against class is a political struggle".[19]

Max Weber on Class —Max Weber, like Marx, asserts that the economic organization of society is the basis of social class. People are in the same class situation, Weber says, when their occupation or their ownership of property gives them a similar chance, however large or small, to obtain some of the things valued in society; material good, physical health, education, travel, leisure and exposure to a wide range of highly prized social experiences. Some people have goods to sell to others, and it is this which determines their life—chances. Other people sell their labour on a labour market to available employers. Still others, such as professionals, offer highly valued and relatively scarce services to a clientele. Each of these constitutes a different "class situation". For Weber, a class is a collectivity of people who share a common set of life-chances as these are determined by property, occupation, and income. His specific definition is, "we may speak of a "class" when (1) a number of people have in common a specific casual component of their life-chances, insofar as (2) this component is represented exclusively by economic interests in the possession of goods and the opportunity for income, and (3) is represented under the conditions of the commodity or labor markets."[20]

For both Marx and Weber, then social classes are outcomes of unequal social reward that are successfully claimed by various economic strata for their participation in the productive processes of the society.

The phenomenon of social classes has always been a matter of great interest to social thinkers of all ages, but with a difference. Most ancient social thinkers both in the West (Aristotle) and the East (Manu), sang it to testify and rationalize the existing social divisions and inequality in terms of a general metaphysical-religious-mythological theory of social stratification, viewing caste and class divisions as "natural" or divinely ordained and thus something not, to be tempered with. But the modern approach to the phenomenon of social class and social stratification (Ougyburn and Nimkoff regulated inequality) is scientific and secular, that is, sociological, also, inequality is now treated as a disvalue, as something which ought to be and can be reduced or even completely eliminated.[21]

INCOME PER MONTH

The present economic system not only introduces new methods but also initiates changes in the forms of social and structural value orientation, motivation and norms of people.

Table 5.7

Monthly Income of University and Degree College Teachers

Income Group	*University Level Teachers (M/F)*	*%*	*College Level Teachers (M/F)*	*%*	*Total*	*%*
Lower Class						**(5.33%)**
0-1000	0	0	5	3.33	5	1.67
1000-2000	6	4	5	3.33	11	3.68
Middle Class						**(49.33%)**
2000-4000	3	2	0	0	3	1
4000-6000	41	27.34	49	32.67	90	30
6000-8000	18	12	37	24.67	55	18.33
Upper Class						**(45.33%)**
8000-10,000	17	11.33	20	13.33	37	12.33
10,000-12,000	15	10	22	14.67	37	12.33
12,000-14,000	32	21.33	8	5.33	40	13.33
14,000 and above	18	12	4	2.67	22	7.33

The Table 5.7 shows that most of the teachers are from middle class (49.33%) and 45.33% teachers belong to the upper class and only 5.33% teachers were from the lower class. Many sociologists and thinkers describe the class but they can't distribute these classes and this is not significant division of class in the sociology, hence we cannot distribute these teachers into specific class.

ACADEMIC RECORDS

Durkheim defined education as the action exercised by the older generation upon those who are not yet ready for social life. Its object is to awaken and develop in the child those physical, intellectual and moral states which are required of him both by his society as a whole and by the milieu for which he is specially destined.[22] This action, the socialization of new generations necessarily takes place in all societies but it assumed many different forms in respect of the social groups and institutions involved, and in respect of its own diversity and complexity.

So far I have been largely concerned with educational differentiation, that is, with the transmission of younger generations of different codes of behaviour largely influenced by social class. But as Durkheim observed, education also prepares the child for life in society as a whole, by transmitting common social traditions through the language, religion, morals and customs of the society. The inculcation of national values has been especially apparent in modern societies and was for long reflected in the social prestige of teachers.

In ancient India the status of a teacher always remained very high. He has been called the "Guru" commanding deep respect not only of pupils but also of parents and the entire society. Thus the profession of teaching has been considered a scared mission. Teacher's good academic record is a major factor to develop his teaching skills. At present academic career of teachers is more important in the field of selection and their promotion. The present study have covered three faculties of university and its associated degree colleges that is Arts, Commerce and Science.

Table 5.8
Academic Records of University and Degree College Teachers

Academic Records	*University Level Teachers (M/F)*	*%*	*College Level Teachers (M/F)*	*%*	*Total*	*%*
M.A.	107	71.33	70	46.67	177	59
M.Sc.	32	21.33	55	36.67	87	29
M.Com.	11	7.34	5	16.66	36	12
Ph.D.	130	86.67	120	80	250	83.33
D. Litt.	23	15.33	8	5.33	31	10.33
Diploma	9	6	12	8	21	7
Gold Medalist	22	14.67	13	8.69	35	11.67

Table 5.8 reveals the most teachers are from the faculty of Arts 59% and Ph.D. degree holders teachers percentage is greater than D. Litt. (10.33%), Diploma (7%) and Gold medalist (11.67%). The table also reveals it that most Ph.D. degree holder teachers are from the University level (83.33%). Its reason is that they have more facilities of research work in comparison of college teachers.

FINDINGS

The data regarding the bio-data of the teachers reveal useful information about them. Male and female teachers have a equal number in the present study from university and college level. Maximum number of teachers belonged to age group of 20 to 40 years. This shows that the teachers of university and its associated degree colleges are young one. Data regarding religion and caste remained according to expectation when representation of Hindus, Muslims and Christians. Most teachers are from Hindu community and upper castes, lower caste or backward caste position is lower in the present data. Teaching profession in the University is dominated by upper castes Hindu Brahmins (48.66%) and upper casts Muslims Sayed (39%). About professional rank a high percentage of teachers (43%) were Readers and 40% were Lecturers (5.66% temporary and 34.33% permanent Lecturers). The percentage of Professors has only 16.66% because professors are available only from the University of Lucknow. The data regarding the family structure of teachers, maximum number of teachers belonged to nuclear families 81% teachers comes from the nuclear families and only 19% teachers have joint families. About marital status a greater percentage of teachers, 66.6% were married while only 19.6% teachers were found to be single 6.6% teachers were divorcee and 7% were widow in the present study. In India teacher's professional conditions are not working good and economically this profession is not very lucrative, the present investigation shows that 49% teachers were from the middle class and 45% were from the upper class and only 5% teachers are from the lower background. Good academic career helps to build up the profession of teaching. Data regarding the academic background of teachers shows that 100% teachers have their essential qualification (Masters' Degree), 83.33% teachers have D.Litt. Degree, 7% have diploma course and 11.67% teachers were gold medalist.

NOTES

1. Khalil, Gibran, *The Prophet. William Human*, L.T.P. Mattoume London (1956 Edition).
2. Arun P. Bali, *College Teachers—challenges and response*.
3. S.N. Mukherji, *Education in India. Today and tomorrow*, Baroda, Acharya Book Depot, 1957, pp. 201-202.
4. Mannheim, Karl, *Ideology and Utopia*, London, Routledge and Kegan Paul, 1936, p. 50.
5. Eleanor Maccoby, (ed.) The *Development of Sex Differences*, Stanford, Cali. Stanford University Press, 1966.
6. Michelle Zimbalist Rosaldo and Louise Lamphese, "Introduction"

to their edited Women, Culture and Society (Stanford University Press, 1974). p.5.

7. Sherwood L. Washburn and C.S. Lancaster, "The Evolution of Hunditng," in Richard B-Lee and Irven Devorse eds. *Man the Hunter* (Chicago: Aldine, 1968), p. 293.

8. See Talcott Parsons and Robert Bales, (eds.) *Family Socialization and interaction process*. (New York, The Free Press, 1955).

9. Maccoby and Jacklin, *op. cit*.

10. *Women Culture and Society: A Theoretical Overview*, in Rosaldo and Lamphere, op. cit., p. 17-43.

11. This Section is adopted from Langermann and Wallace (1985: 141-144). See George Ritzer, *Sociological Theory*, McGraw Hill, INC. Internatinal Editions, 1992.

12. Chanchal Sarkar, *The Unquiet Campus*, New Delhi, 1960, p. 12.

13. Lawson, E.T. and MacCauley, R.N., *Rethinking Religion: connecting Cognition and Cultrure*, Cambridge University Press, Cambridge, 1990.

14. Srinivas, M.N., *Religion and Society among the Coorgs of South India*, Oxford University Press, Oxford, 1952.

15. Durkheim, E, *The Elementry Forms of Religious Life*, Allen and Unwia, London, 1976.

16. Kumari Pritima, *Changing Values among Young Women*, Delhi, Amar Prakashan, 1988. p. 4.

17. MacIver and C.H. Page, *Society: an Introducto analysis*, Rinehart, 1949.

18. Karl Marx, The Eighteenth Brumaire of Louis Bonaparte, Marx and Engels, *Selected Works*, Moscow, Progress Publishers, 1968.

19. Karl Marx, The Poverty of Philosophy, New York, International Publishers.

20. Max Weber, "Class, Status and Party" in Hans Gerth and C. Wrigth Mills, from Max Weber, *Essays in Sociology* (New York, Oxford University Press, 1946, p. 181.

21. Ogburn, W.F. and M.F. Nimkoff, *Technology and the Changing Family*, Bosten, N. York Houghten Mifflin Co., 1955.

22. E. Durkheim, *Education et. sociologic* (Paris), 1922.

REFERENCES

1. Marini, Margaret M, Sociology of Gender, in E.F. Borgatta and K.S. Cook (eds.), *The Future of Sociology*, Beverly Hills, Calif; Sage, 1988.
2. Mackinnon, Catherine, *Sexual Harassment of Working Women*, New Haven: Yale University Press, 1979.
3. Langermann, Patricia Madoo, "The Founding of the American Sociological Review", *American Sociological Review*, 1979.
4. Laws, Judith Long, and Schwartz, Pepper, *Sexual Scripts: The Social Construction of Female Sexuality* Hinsdale, Ill, Dryden, 1977.
5. Mitchell, Juliet, *Psychoanalysis and Feminism*, New York, 1975.
6. Bernard, Jessie, *Women and the Public Interest*, Chicago, Aldine, 1983.
7. Bernard Jessie, *The Female World*, New York, Free Press, 1981.
8. Cardon, Maren Lockwood, *The New Feminist Movement*, New York Russel, Sage R. , 1974.
9. Baltzel, E. Digby, *Philadelphia Gentlemen: The making of a National Upper Class*, Free Press of Glencoe, New York, 1958.
10. Bendix, Reinhard, and Seymour Lipset (Eds.); *Class, Status and Power*, The Free Press of Glencoe, New York, 1966.
11. C. Wright Mills, *The Power Elite*, New York, Oxford University Press, 1965.
12. Ralph Dahrendorf, *Class and Class Conflict in Industrial Society*, Stanford, Cal. Stanford University Press, 1959.
13. Frank Parkin, *Class, Inequality and Political Order; Social Stratification in Capitalist and Communist Societies*, New York, Praeger Publishers, 1971.

Chapter 6

Family Setting

Family patterns show a fascinating variation from society to society, and persons from one society who become involved in the family patterns of a different society generally react in a predictably ethnocentric manner. Why, if the family is so important, has mankind been unable to find and agree upon some ideal pattern of family life which best serves human needs?

In the most primitive societies, the family is the only institution. Among the polar Eskimos, there are no other institutions—no chiefs or formal laws, no priests or medicine men, no specialized occupations. Within the family all the business of living is fulfilled. In other words, they have no physical or social needs that call for an institutional structure other than that provided by their family.

As a culture grows more complex, its institutional structures become more elaborate. The family is an adequate structure for handling the economic production and consumption of primitive hunters and farmers. But what happens when they develop trade with neighbouring or distant tribes? Before long the group includes traders, shippers, and other specialists whose work is no longer a part of the family life of the society. Later, specialized craftsmen begin to produce trade goods, giving rise to further occupational differentiation. Economic institutions exist whenever economic functions are performed in routing ways by specialists, operating outside their family roles and functions.

In the most primitive societies, order is maintained with no formal laws, police, or courts. The only authority known in many simple societies is family authority; that is certain family members have certain authority over others. With increasing tribal size and growing cultural complexity, more formal political organization is needed. Family heads are joined into tribal councils, tribes combine into confederations, and bureaucracies begin to develop. Welfare, in both primitive and modern societies, is a powerful stimulus to political organization, for only through political organization can an aroused rabble be mobilized for an effective military effort. In like manner, religious and educational institutions develop as professional functionaries, following standardized procedure, and withdraw from the family certain activities too complicated for the family to handle well. Like all institutions, the family is a system of accepted norms and procedures for getting some importing jobs done. The family is defined as a *kinship grouping which provides for the rearing of children for certain other human needs.* If a society is to survive, people must find some workable and dependable ways of pairing off, conceiving and raising children, and fulfilling the other functions of the family.

The family in any society is an institutional structure which develops through a society's efforts to get certain tasks done. What are the tasks commonly performed through the family?

The family is the principal institution through which societies organize and regulate the satisfaction of sexual desires. Most societies provide some alternative sexual outlets. With varying degree of indulgence, each society also tolerates some sex behaviour in violation of its norms. But all societies expect that most sexual intercourse will occur between persons whom their institutional norms define as legitimately accessible to each other. These norms sometimes allow for considerable sexual variety; yet no society is entirely promiscuous. In every society there are mores which forbid certain persons access to one another. What may look to us like promiscuity is more likely to be complicated system of sexual permissions and taboos which we do not fully understand.

Every society depends primarily upon the family for the business of producing children. Other arrangements are theoretically possible, and many societies arrange to accept children produced outside a marriage relationship. But no society has established a set of norms for providing children except as part of a family.

All societies depend primarily upon the family for the socialization of children into adults who can function successfully in that society. Thinkers from Plato to Huxley (1932; 1958) have speculated about other arrangements, and dozens of experiments in communal child rearing have been attempted and abandoned. The family is the child's family primary group, and this is where his personality development begins. By the time he is old enough to enter primary groupings outside the family, the basic foundations of his personality are already firmly laid.

In all societies the family other some degree of physical, economic, psychological protection to its members. In many societies any attack on persons is an attack upon his entire family, with all members bound to defend him or to revenge the injury. In most primitive societies the family is extended food-sharing unit which starves or flattens together; as long as a man's relatives have food, he has no fear of hunger. And in many primitive society as in ours, very few persons outside one's family really care what happens to him.

The family has become a major conceptual tool of sociological research and analysis. The significance of family lies, according to Cooley, in the being the "primary" agency of socialization or, as Friend would have it, development of "Super-ego". But two things must be noted: First , the family has lost many of its earlier functions in modern industrial - urban society, including socialization function: "...the family" observes Worsely, "is not such a central agency of socialization in our society as it has been at other times and in other societies."[1]

Secondly, the most important question about family's socialization function is "Socialization into what?. That is, it will not be enough to merely analyse the process and mechanism of socialization as such attention has also to be focused on the content of socialization. With this connection it will not be wrong to say that the context of socialization, that is, the norms and values and behaviour pattern inculcated in the child by the family, are basically those of the larger society. In the transitional stage characterized by uneven change in the different sectors or society however, the family norms may be in conflict with those of the wider society.

SIBLING POSITION

In India and other countries too eldest son is given more importance and allotted more privileges. He shares major part of ancestral property, while others may be deprived of them. Shariat laws among Muslims lay down provisions of bigger share for male children and smaller for daughters. But the daughters are not deprived of their shares even after their marriage.

Table 6.1

University and Degree College Teacher Sibling Position

Position	*University Level* Number	%	*College Level* Number	%	*Total*	%
Only Child	11	7.1	11	7.3	22	7.33
Elder Child	60	40.1	49	32.7	109	36.34
Middle Child	41	27.3	40	26.7	81	27
Youngest Child	38	25.3	50	33.3	88	29.33
Total	50	100	150	100	300	100

Table 6.1 shows that, 7.33% were the only child of their parents. Elder children of their parents among the teacher were 36.34%. Middle children of their father and mothers were 27%. Percentage of the youngest children among their brothers and sisters of teachers was 29.33%.

PARENTAL MAKE-UP

Parents have a very important role in the personality formation of children. They occupy the highest position in family structure. As family is very significant unit of society, parents are significant units in family. The entire social action and interaction which an individual does, is taught by parents. Parents play a responsible role in making and casting of personality of an individual. All tracts which are visible in a child. In fact those are inspired and caught by parents. In most of the cases the future of an individual is guided and organized by parents. Living parents are matchless assets and guiding hands for individual.

Table 6.2

Parental Make-up of University and Degree College Teachers

Parental Make-up	*University Level* *Number*	*%*	*College Level* *Number*	*%*	*Total*	*%*
Father alive Mother alive	45	30	40	26.7	85	28.3
Father dead Mother alive	65	43.3	70	46.7	135	45.0
Father alive Mother dead	22	14.7	25	16.6	47	15.7
Father dead Mother dead	18	12	15	10	33	11.0
Total	50	100	150	100	300	100

Data in Table 6.2 lay down that in most of the cases 45% teachers' father was died and mother alive while 28.3% teachers' parents were alive and 15.7% teachers' father was alive and mothers were died. The most unfortunate cases where mother and father both have died were 11 per cent.

PARENTS EDUCATIONAL STATUS

Education is very significant variable. It decides social status of individual's education as it has been playing important role in almost all aspects of human life. It plays a decisive part in the placement of the worker's in the society. Parents education adds a lot to education of the children. They can guide the education of their issues in the right direction. As the role of mother is more important, therefore, education for ladies (mother) has been much emphasized.

Table 6.3

Parents Educational Status of University and Degree College Teachers

Educational Status	*University Level Number*	*%*	*College Level Number*	*%*	*Total*	*%*
(A) Father						
Primary	17	11.2	32	21.3	49	16.4
Middle		22	14.6	40	26.7	20.6
Higher	80	53.6	45	30.0	125	41.6
Professional	31	20.6	33	22.0	64	21.4
Total	150	100	150	100	300	100
(B) Mother						
Illiterate	7	4.7	4	2.7	11	3.7
Primary	38	25.3	60	40.0	98	32.7
Middle	42	28.0	37	24.7	66	26.3
Higher	40	26.7	26	17.3	66	22.0
Professional	23	15.3	23	15.3	46	15.3
Total	50	100	150	100	300	100

Table 6.3 shows the educational status of respondents' parents. It shows that 16.4% teachers father were primary educated and 20.6% fathers were middle level educated. 41.6% fathers of teachers were highly educated and 21.4% father of respondents had professional qualifications (doctors,

lawyers, engineers, business man, farmers etc.). The present data shows that the educational status of the teachers mother was of course lower than their fathers education. 3.7% teachers mother were illiterate, 32.7% mothers were primary level education, 26.3% teachers' mother were middle level educated and 22% teachers' mother were highly educated. The percentage of professional education in case of mothers the obtained percentage was 15.3 per cent.

PATTERN OF SPENDING VACATION

This brings us to the significant aspect of teachers' relation with their families, namely, the pattern of spending their vacations. It is obvious that university and college, if taken seriously, is almost a whole time pursuit, which keeps these teachers busy with teaching additives all the year round in one form or the other. As a result teachers may not get much time to give their families.

Table 6.4

University and Degree College Teachers Pattern of Spending Vacation

Pattern of Spending Vacation	*University Level* *Number*	*%*	*College Level* *Number*	*%*	*Total*	*%*
With Family	115	`76.7	105	70	220	73.3
With Friends	35	23.3	45	30	80	26.7
Total	150	`100	150	100	300	100

Table 6.4 reveals that 73.7% teachers spent their vacations with their families and 26.3% teachers spent their vacations with friends.

VISIT TO FAMILY MEMBERS

The joint families future are in dark at present time, there are so many factors behind most teachers have nuclear family but they visit their relatives and family members houses, as the present study shows.

Table 6.5
Visit to Family Members by the University and Degree College Teachers

Visits	*University Level* *Number*	*%*	*College Level* *Number*	*%*	*Total*	*%*
Regularly	47	31.3	30	20.0	77	25.6
Occasionally	65	43.3	85	56.7	150	50.0
Infrequently	30	20.0	21	14.0	51	17.0
Never	8	5.4	14	9.3	22	7.4
Total	150	100	150	100	300	100

Table 6.5 reveals that 25.6% teachers visit to their family members houses regularly, 50% teachers visit occasionally, 17% infrequently visit to relatives and only 7.4% teachers never visit to family members.

CHANGE IN FAMILY PATTERN

Change is a universal phenomenon and there can exist no society without change. Man's life itself is a good example of change. Together with the change in different ages, there were also changes in the wants and needs of the human beings.

Table 6.6
Changes in Family of University and Degree College Teachers

Changes in Family	*University Level* *Number*	*%*	*College Level* *Number*	*%*	*Total*	*%*
Yes	109	72.7	99	66	208	69.3
No	41	27.3	51	34	92	30.7
Total	150	100	150	100	300	100

Table 6.6 shows that 69% teachers says that they make changes in the family as a head of the family and 30.2% teachers were not make any type of change in the family pattern.

RESISTANCE AGAINST CHANGE

In India we are presently passing through a crucial period of social change as never before. Traditional India becoming modern and education play today as a powerful instrument for social change. Our Constitution provided equality and social freedom to every citizen. Every citizen is an important unit of society. So we can't forced them to any type of change.

Table 6.7 reveals that 33.3% teachers elders resist the change in the family and 29.7% teacher's youngers resist the change. Present study shows that 22.3% teacher's elders and youngers both resist the change and only 14.7% teachers family members did not resist the changes in the family pattern.

Table 6.7

Resistance Against Change by University and Degree College Teachers Family Members

Resistance Change Against	*University Level Number*	*%*	*College Level Number*	*%*	*Total*	*%*
Elders	55	36.7	45	130	100	33.3
Youngers	40	26.7	49	32.7	89	29.7
Both	36	24.0	31	20.7	67	22.3
None of Them	19	12.6	25	16.6	44	14.7
Total	150	100	150	100	300	100

TRADITION PATTERN IN THE FAMILY

India is basically a traditional country. Traditions has played a very important role in shaping the life attitudes, behaviour and various activities of human beings. Tradition is related to every one's life whether he may be a ruler or a ruled, teachers or the taught. There can exist no society without a tradition and custom.

Table 6.8

Tradition Pattern of University and Degree College Teachers Family

Pattern of Family Tradition	*University Level Number*	*%*	*College Level Number*	*%*	*Total*	*%*
(i) Comparatively Same	5	3.3	7	4.7	12	4
(ii) Slightly Changed	52	34.7	75	50.0	127	42.3
(iii) Comparatively Changed	57	38.0	45	30	102	34.0
(iv) Moderate	31	20.7	15	10	46	15.4
(v) Ultra Moderate	5	3.3	8	5.3	13	4.3
Total	150	100	150	100	300	100

The present data from Table 6.8 reveals that 4% teachers have comparatively same pattern of tradition in the family, 42.3% teachers have slightly changed pattern, 34% have comparatively changed in the pattern of family tradition, 15.2% have moderate pattern of family and 4.3% teachers have ultra moderate family pattern.

MEMBERS IN THE FAMILY

Family is such a primary unit or a group of society where members are directly related share woes and joys of one another, yet differences among them may also a be sorted possibly of the fact that all members of the family are smoothly related and share joys and sorrows. Family is a first primary agency of socialization. At present, the idea of joint families is not working successfully, as the present study indicates that, most of the university and degree college teachers came from nuclear families (See Table 6.5).

Table 6.9

Distribution of Members in the Family of University and Degree College Teachers

Members	*University Level* *Number*	*%*	*College Level* *Number*	*%*	*Total*	*%*
Male**						
i. One	100	69.4	90	60	190	64.6
ii. Two	25	17.4	45	30	70	23.8
iii. More than Two	19	13.2	15	10	34	11.6
Total	144	100	0150	100	294	100
Female**						
i. One	90	60	65	43.3	455	51.7
ii. Two	35	23.3	55	36.7	90	30.0
iii. More than Two	25	16.7	30	20	55	18.3
Total	150	100	150	100	300	100
Child**						
i. One	70	41.9	65	61.9	135	49.6
ii. Two	80	47.9	30	28.6	110	40.4
iii. More than Two	17	10.2	10	9.5	27	10
Total	167	100	105	100	272	100

The Table 6.9 shows that the percentage of one male is more 64.6% than two and three male members. In case of female family members one female is more (51.7) than two and three females. The percentage of one child is more (49.6) than two and three childrens. Hence we can say that most teachers have a small family with one or two child.

EARNING MEMBERS

Investigation regarding the earning members in the family of the respondents shows in most of the cases two persons were as a earning members in the families of university and college teachers.

Table 6.10
Earning Members in University and Degree College Teachers Families

Earning Members	*University Level* *Number*	*%*	*College Level* *Number*	*%*	*Total*	*%*
One	47	31.3	40	40	107	35.6
Two	86	57.3	60	40	146	48.7
More than Two	17	11.4	30	20	47	15.7
Total	150	100	0150	100	300	100

Present table exhibits that 35.6% teachers had single earning members in the family. 48.7% teachers had two earning members in the family and 15.6% teachers of the sample had more than two persons in the family.

LIFE PARTNER'S PROFESSION

Education will be used as agent of basic change in the status of women. In order to neutralize the accumulated distortions of the past, there will be a well-conceived edge in favour of women. The national education system will play a positive interventionist role in the empowerment of women. It will foster the development of new values through redesigned curricula, text books, the training and orientation of teachers decision-makers and administrative and the active involvement of educational institutions. This will be an act of faith and social engineering. Women's studies will be promoted as a part of various courses and educational institutions encouraged to take up active programs, to further women's development. The removal of women's illiteracy and obstacles inhibiting their access to, and retention in, elementary education will receive overriding priority through provision of special support services, setting of time targets, and effective monitoring. Major emphasis will be laid on women's participation in vocational, technical and professional education at different levels. The policy of non-discrimination will be pursued vigorously to eliminate sex stereotyping in vocational and professional courses and to promote women's participation in non-traditional occupations, as well as existing and emergent technologies. [2]

Table 6.11

Profession of the University and Degree College Teacher's Life Partner

Profession	University Level Number	%	College Level Number	%	Total	%
Teaching	48	36.3	35	26.9	83	31.7
Non-Teaching	38	28.8	35	36.9	73	27.8
House Wife	46	34.9	60	46.2	106	40.5
Total	132	100	130	100	262	100

Above table reveals that 31.7% teacher's life partners were in teaching profession and 27.8% teachers were not in teaching profession. Table also reveals that 40.5% teachers life partner did not have any job they were housewives.

FINDINGS

Investigations regarding the family setting of university and degree college teachers revealed certain interesting facts. Most of the teachers (36.33%) were the eldest child of their parents. A majority of teachers (45%) had lost their fathers but their mother was alive. The present study shows that the percentage of respondent's father's educational qualification was high in comparison of their mother's qualifications, illiteracy percentage was related only from the mother case, there were 3.7% respondent's mother was illiterate and 41.6% teachers father was highly educated and 21.4% teacher's father were professionally educated. The percentage of highly educated mothers was 22% and professionally educated percentage was 15.3%. The available data reveals that 63.3% teachers spend their vacations with family and 26.7% spend their vacation with their friends. 50% teachers visit to their family members or relatives houses occasionally, it is a maximum score; 25.6% teachers visit to family members regularly, 17% infrequently and only 7% teachers never visit to family members. To collect the information about change, only 14.3% teachers elders and youngers did not resist the changes in the family. The data regarding the tradition pattern of teacher's family the respondents reveals useful information about them. 4% teachers have comparatively same pattern of family as their parents have earlier, 42.3% teachers have slightly changed traditional pattern in the family, 34% teachers have comparatively changed pattern of family, 15.4% teachers have moderate pattern in their families. The data regarding the members in family reveals that the percentage of one male and one female is high in comparison of two or more than two males and females. It shows that most teachers had a nuclear family background. 64.6% were the single male (man) of their families and 51.7% were the single female (woman) of their families. The percentage of one child was 49.6% and 40.4% teachers had two children and only 10% teachers had more than two children in the family. The data regarding the earning members in the family shows that 35.6% teachers had only one earning members (self) in the family while the percentage of two earning members was 48.7% and 15.7% teachers have more than two earning members in the family. To collect the information regarding the profession of teacher's life partner, these findings were obtained 31.7% teachers life partners have teaching profession, 27.8% teacher's life partners have non- teaching professions and 40.5% teachers life partner were housewives.

REFERENCES & NOTES

1. Peter Worsley et al., *Introducing Sociology*, p. 141.
2. National Policy on Education, Ministry of Human Resource Development, Government of India, Department of Education, May, 1986.

3. MurDock George P, *Social Structure*, The Macmillan Company, New York, 1949.
4. Queen Stuart, A Robert W. Habenstein, and John B. Adams, *The Family in Various Culture*, J.B. Lippincott Company, Philadelphia, 1952, 1961, 1962.
5. Reiss, Ira, L., *Pre-maritul Sexual Standards in America*, The Free Press of Glencoe, New York, 1960.
6. Schur, Edwin, Me. (Ed.), *The Family and the Sexual Revolution*, Indiana Press, Bloomington, Ind; 1964.
7. Paul B. Horton and Chestor L. Hunt, *Sociology*, Second Edition, McGraw Hill Inc., 1964.

Chapter 7

Professional Organisational Setup

Education today is a powerful instrument for social change. The term education has been given specific connotations. Education helps in the development of rational powers of man, the physical and the social environment in a scientific sense. The importance of a teacher in the educational process is questionable, however, the entire edifice of education is shaky if the teacher is weak and ineffective. An effective teacher is amongst the foremost factors contributing to educational importance, which we are trying hard to achieve.

Indian Higher education is the first largest in the world, with 1,69,615 teachers in the university system and with a student intake of 2,43,150 in 1980. In India, the college teaching profession emerged under colonialism and reflected many of the values of the British Colonial System (Gilbert, 1972). There are, thus two categories of university teachers those who are employees of universities and teach either one of the teaching universities or at the university departments of federal and affiliating universities. And those who are employees of college and teachers of constituent or affiliated college. College teachers working in undergraduate institutions constitute 80% of the academic community in India, while university teachers constitute only a small part of this community. Generally speaking university teachers have better remuneration, better working conditions, office facilities, some secretarial assistance and have housing or other fringe benefits, and enjoy a higher professional status when compared to college teachers. Teachers in the college have hardly any control over their conditions of work teaching schedules or other aspects of everyday academic life. They are expected to follow curriculum, and a set of policies and rules most of which determined by various colleges and universities in their classroom is conditioned by several factors such as the various universities requirements, evaluation of student performance by the university, and influence of the national educational system over instructional materials. University professors on the other hand, are small in number and work in an atmosphere which is different from the colleges, but it is generally they who set the standards and provide role models for college teachers to follow (Altbach, 1977).

There is relatively low scope for upward mobility within the Indian academic profession. Promotion opportunities are generally inadequate. Lack of promotional prospects tends to act as a deterrent for many talented persons from joining the teaching profession. It has also become a serious grievance for many teachers and over the years it has become a major factor of teachers discontentment. This observation has been repeatedly made by several inquiry committees, such as the Second Education Commission (1966), set up by the Government of India, the Sen Committee (1973), appointed by the UGC, and the Mathur Committee (1981), which was set up by the University of Delhi.

POLITICAL WING IN PROFESSIONAL SETUP

The attitude towards teachers' participation in politics has however, changed since Independence. The traditionalist political essayist like Hannah Arendt treat this very loss of authority as the crux of the present education crisis.

Table 7.1
Political Wing in the University and Degree College Teachers' Professional Setup

Political Wing in Professional Setup	*University Level Number*	*%*	*College Level Number*	*%*	*Total*	*%*
Yes	47	31.3	20	13.3	67	22.33
No	103	68.7	130	86.7	233	77.67
Total	150	100	150	100	300	100

The present study confirms the fact that the Indian teacher is not at all political. The overwhelming majority of teachers (77.6%) said that there were not a political wing in their educational institutions and 22.3% said that they had a political wing in the professional setup (See Table 7.1).

WORSHIP PLACE IN THE INSTITUTION

Religion describes human values, ideals, cultural traditions, moral conduct for the human society. There exist many religious background in this country and people developed culture freely in this background of religions. In the ancient days religion occupied a very important place in the human right. It was the main inspiration for the education. In those days a man was expected to think act study and live according to instructions given in the religion books. Education was completely linked by religion. Even during the medieval period educational institutions were housed in churches, temples, mosques, Buddha Vihar's and Mathas were virtually schools.

Table 7.2
Any Worship Place in the University and Degree Colleges Teachers' Professional Setup

Worship Places	*University Level Number*	*%*	*College Level Number*	*%*	*Total*	*%*
Yes	0	-	0	-	-	-
No	150	100	150	100	300	100
Total	150	100	150	100	300	100

Above Table 7.2 reveals that all universities and degree college teachers said that there is not any worship place in their educational institutions.

DEMAND OF DONATION FOR WORSHIP PLACES IN EDUCATIONAL INSTITUTIONS

Table 7.2 reveals that there is not a single place in the educational institution hence the percentage of demand for the donation of money to maintain the worship places was also nil. All teachers from university and degree level said that don't donate some fixed amount for the worship places (situated in educational institutions).

Table 7.3

Demand of Donation for Worship Places in Educational Institutions

Political Wing in Professional Setup	*University Level Number*	*%*	*College Level Number*	*%*	*Total*	*%*
Yes	-	-	-	-	-	-
No	150	100	150	150	300	100
Total	150	100	150	100	300	100

Above table exhibits that there were not a single person who donate for the worship places. Because they don't had any religious place in their educational institution.

INTEGRATION : A MAJOR RECENT PROBLEM OF INDIA

In a nation like India where pupil with different religions, caste, creeds and languages live national integration is of paramount importance for the security of the country. Although variety enriches and helps the development of a country but misguide and unscrupulous hence some times threaten the very existence of the nation. India unfortunately is passing through a difficult phase at present. The country is plagued by the evils of linguism, communalism, sectarianism, provincialism, regionalism, terrorism and some other evils. We have eccepted democracy and as such we have to give recognition to diversities, but we have to ensure that there is unity in diversity and diversity does not get an upper hand to the extent that it strikes at the very root of occasional communal riots, language controversy etc. are such happenings which indicate that the nation is not proceeding on the right path of national integration.

A teacher has been given a key position in the educational process of the country, because education is the most powerful medium of the achievement for national integration. It provides the necessary inspiration and all those (teachers, students) who are concerned with education should keep in mind that we have to achieve national integration through the education of masses.

Table 7.4

Discussion on National Integration Problems by the University and College Teachers

Discussions	*University Level*		*College Level*		*Total*	*%*
	Number	*%*	*Number*	*%*		
Yes	132	88	140	93.3	272	90.7
No	18	112	10	6.7	28	9.3
Total	150	100	150	300	100	

Table 7.4 exhibits that a majority of 90.7% university and college teachers said that they discuss national integration problems among their staff members in their institutions and only 9.3% teachers do not discuss these major recent problems. Hence we can say that mostly these agent of social change are aware about national integrations.

CASTE FEELING IN EDUCATIONAL SETUP

In Indian context, caste play a major role in the educational setup. For in spite of much social change and modernization, therefore is hardly any organization—economic, political, administrative and educational[1] in which caste considerations do not play some and at times a major role. Many observers and analysts of the university highlighted the impact of caste on university affairs. For example, Chanchal Sarkar observes, "caste and community still remain troublesome, inhibiting factors in the university." In Mysore where the entire machinery is geared to caste, it is not surprising that caste should play powerful role among both teachers and students.[2]

Table 7.5

Caste Feeling in University and Degree College Teachers Institutions

Caste Feeling	*University Level* Number	%	*College Level* Number	%	*Total*	%
Yes	27	18	30	20	57	19
No	123	82	120	80	243	81
Total	150	100	150	100	300	100

Table 7.5 reveals that 19% teachers said that they feel caste feeling in their institution and among staff members, but a majority of teachers (81%) said that there is not a caste feeling in educational institutions where they work.

FINDINGS

The data regarding the professional organizational setup of the respondents reveal useful information about them. Maximum number of teachers said that there is not a political wing in their professional setup while 77.3% teachers said it, and only 22.3% feel that there is a political wing in their organizational set up. Data regarding the worship places and donation of money for the worship places reveals that 100% teachers don't donate money for the worship places because they do not have any religious place in their educational institutions. National integration is a major recent problem for the Indian national and emotional unity. As a agent of social change it is moral duty of a teacher that he must discuss these problems, and suggests solution to remove these evils. A majority of teachers (90.7%) said that they discuss on national integration problems and 9.3% said that they do not discuss on it with the staff members. Religion and caste is a major factor in the educational setup. The present study shows that 19% teachers said there is a caste feeling in the educational and in their organizational setup, while 81% said there is not a caste feeling in their professional institutions.

REFERENCES

1. Sen Verma, *The National Herald*, October 9, 1971.
2. Chanchal Sarkar, *The Unquiet Campus*, New Delhi, 1960, p.12.

Chapter 8

Activism and Political Background

Political parties, Max Weber once said, live in a house of power. Whatever else politics is about, it is about power.

To speak of power often evokes in us unpleasant images: of the few who rule and the many who are ruled; of special interests and privileged classes; of bosses and dictators; and of the struggle of class against class. But the political process also includes the actions of democratic citizens, who were the majority decide and the authority of law commands respect and obedience.

In traditional, preindustrial societies, the political process often is only partially differentiated from the religion's and economic process, and political authority is embedded in customs and traditions of ancient origin. But in modern society the political process has developed specialized structure and roles, and authority is legally specified in charters, constitutins, and by-laws.

Among social scientists there is an increasing tendency to define power in terms of group or societal decision-making, from that perspective, power is a social process, not an object or "thing" divided among power-holders. To have power is to participate in a decision making. To be powerful is to control decision-making in a group or atleast have a very strong influence on what decisions are made. To be powerless, in turn, is to be excluded from decision–making.

Power can not be understood apart from authority. When a Prime Minister of our Secular Democratic India vetoes a bill, he exercises the authority of his office, as does the legislature when it votes on a bill. Authority is legitimate power the right to make a decision that is based on an acceptance of the claims of decision-makers that their decisions are binding on all members as the social organization involved.

Max Weber has indicated that in stable social orders the legitimacy of authority may be traditional, as the authority of village elders or a tribal chief, rooted in custom and cultural traditions, or it may be legal-rational as in modern societies, derived from documents (Laws, Charters and Constitutions). In situtation of instability and change, authority is often charismatic; that is, based upon the personal devotion of the followers or leader, who attributes to him the great qualities.[1] When this happens, masses of people no longer accept the traditional or legal-rational system of authority as legitimate.

Yet others besides those with authority do exercise power. In a complex process of reaching decisions others participate when they have access to those have authority. Those who have such access are influentials.

In the modern world almost everyone is a citizen of a nation, and so everyone has a nationality. Yet the process of creating nations is still recent history in Europe and America–note that Germany and Italy only became nations within the last century. Nation-building, furthermore, is a central copmponent of the process of economic development throughout the non-Western World.[2]

Max Weber defined the State as a political organization that claims binding authority and a legitimate monopoly of force within a territory. In the modern nation the state is an inclusive group from which there is no escape. A stateless person belongs nowhere and is, in terms of right and status, a nonperson. All other social groups are subordinate to the authority and the power of the state.

Since the state is the politically dominant and controlling force within a society, with binding authority political struggles in nation are struggle to influence the policies and decisions of the state; they may even be struggle for control of the state of the kinds of groups that organize for this struggle the political party is the most significant. As Weber said, parties "live in a house of 'power' and "are always structures struggling for domination."[3]

The political party originated in England from political clubs that organized to support candidates who, once in office, could reflect the interests and concerns of some citizens more than others. The existence of parties, then, testifies to differences in class and group the richer and the poorer, who want different kinds of political action and differnt kinds of social policies from the state.

Democratic states are, theoretically and constitutionally, multiple-party states, for its citizens have the right to form any party they choose. But among democratic nations there are in fact some varied patterns. Since no single party to have has a majority a coalition of parties to form a government is always necessary.[4] All politicians in democratic societies know that there is a difference among the social classes in both interests among the social classes in both interests and participations in politics. A large quantity of research on political participation seems to confirm what politicians instinctively know that people higher in class position are more likely to participate in politics than are people in lower class. Whether status is measured by income, education or occupation, the result is the same; those of higher status participate more than of those of lower status.[5]

An activist is one who not merely thinks and theorizes but acts to actualize ideas, that is, to give term a practical shape, and activism implies — (i) explicit recognition of the need and desirability of action; and (ii) conscious engagement in action program. This activism begin early in students life. The present study shows that teachers had begun their activism before coming to the university stage.

The major form of the activism are— (i) participating in strikes, demonstrations and protest meetings; (ii) contesting elections in their organizations; (iii) attending conventions and conferences. The first two types or forms of activism are not only the most common, but also disturb the authorities most.

Table 8.1
Participation in Demonstration by the University and Degree College Teachers

Level	*University Level* *Number*	*%*	*College Level* *Number*	*%*	*Total*	*%*
School Level	2	1.3	10	6.7	12	4
College Level	7	46	12	8	19	3
University	3	2	3	2	6	2
Professional	3	3	5	3.3	8	2.6
Total	15		30		45	

Table 8.1 reveals that out of 300 teachers 45 i.e. 11.6 per cent, had taken part in educational demonstration. Now most of these had made their debut in demonstration when they were school level (4%).

HUNGER STRIKE

It was Mahatma Gandhi who forged "fast unto death" as a political weapon during India's freedom struggle against the British Imperialist rule. It therefore continues to be proper with our political activists and protectors of all categories and levels. But the feeling is growing that this method of protest has been much misused since Independence. With the Mahatma, it is pointed out, fast unto death was a matter of "*self purification*", while with most others it is nothing more than a coercive tactic.

Table 8.2

Hunger Strike by the University and Degree College Teachers

Stages	*University Level* Number	%	*College Level* Number	%	*Total*	%
Before coming to the University	6	4	5	3.33	11	3.7
After Joining the University	6	4	2	1.33	8	2.7
At Both Stages	3	4	6	4.0	9	3
Total		15		13		28

It was found in the above table that only 28 of the teachers under study had themselves resorted to hunger strike and that too, at the before university stage. 3.7 per cent and others 2.7 per cent had joined hunger strike at both stages.

Table 8.3

Frequency of University and Degree College Teachers Hunger Strike

Frequency	*University Level* Number	%	*College Level* Number	%	*Total*	%
Once	6	4	5	3.33	11	3.7
Twice	3	2	4	2.7	7	2.33
Thrice	3	2	3	2.4	6	2.0
More than Thrice	3	2	1	0.7	4	1.33
Total		15		13		28

	Number	*Percentage*
Never gone on Hunger Strike	272	90.7

Table 8.3 reveals that 90.7 per cent teachers never gone on hunger strike and 9.3 per cent teachers had gone to hunger strikes, 3.7 per cent teachers had gone once time, 23.33 per cent two times, 2 per cent three times and 1.33 per cent teachers had gone more than three times on hunger strike.

Table 8.4

Election Record of University and Degree College Teachers

Record	*University Level* *Number*	*%*	*College Level* *Number*	*%*	*Total*	*%*
Once	10	6.7	8	5.3	18	7
Twice	3	2.0	3	2.0	6	2
More than two Times	2	1.3	2	1.3	4	1
Total		15		13		28

As table 8.4 reveals that most (7%) teachers had contested the election one time, 2% teachers had contested it two times and 1% teachers had contested the elections more than two times.

Table 8.5

Record of Arrest by the Police for Agitational Activities of University and Degree College Teachers

Stages	*University Level* *Number*	*%*	*College Level* *Number*	*%*	*Total*	*%*
Before Joining the University	8	5.3	9	6	17	15.6
After Joining the University	11	7.3	9	6	20	6.7
Total	19		18		37	

Table 8.5 exhibits that most teachers were arrested by the police before joining the university level (15.6%), and 6.7% teachers were arrested after joining the university. A maximum percentage of teachers 87.7 per cent were never arrested by the police for any agitational activities in the educational institutions, only 12.3 per cent teachers were involve in agitational activities.

PARTICIPATION IN SOCIO-CULTURAL ACTIVITIES

The teacher who is the architect of the new generation has to mould the mind and chisel the behaviour and attitude of the young. Education is comprehensive and synthetic process which aims harmonious development of the body, mind, emotion and spirit of the talent of students. It is necessary for the teaching profession that a teacher should have radical and open mind thinking at a time. The activities and attitudes of a teacher influenced their pupils mind and personality.

Table 8.6

University and Degree College Teachers' Participation in Socio-cultural Activities

Participation	*University Level* *Number*	*%*	*College Level* *Number*	*%*	*Total*	*%*
More	72	48.0	125	83.3	197	65.7
Mild	50	33.3	10	6.7	60	20.0
Never	28	18.7	15	100	43	14.3
Total	150	100	150	100	300	100

Table 8.6 reveals that 65.7 per cent teachers were mostly participated in socio-cultural activities, 20 per cent mildly participated and 14.3 per cent teachers have never attended the socio-cultural activities like seminars, debate, conferences etc. Hence through the analysis we can say that a maximum number of university and college teachers were regularly attending the sociocultural activities.

POLITICAL INTEREST

Politics has become a integral part of the social life. It plays vital role in society. Politics govern the thought of process of individuals. Since most of the countries have opted for democratic form of government, politics has become a necessity. Democracy functions from the roots. It has achieved the shape of tradition. As class representation is very important in an individual's social life, democracy tests class representation. Politics is now a party of our social life. It governs the activities of a man in society. It is also a kind assessment instrument of human beings.

Politics has its role to be performed at very stage. It starts from the very small unit and it has its involvement in higher level too. Then there are political activities of almost all wings of society. People take part in departmental politics election and union. Teachers constitute their union and are always seen very active. Now every stratum of society, even beggars, prostitutes, blind man and bachelors have their organization and take active part in politics. In nut shell it can be understood that politics has lift, no aspect of human life from its impact. Now people try for small politics in very ordinary move of others.

Society and education are interlinked and inter-dependent. Consequently political changes in the society are bound to effect education. Society draws its inspiration from education. It is because of this factor that help of education is sought to give permanent footing to a new political order. Education in India, to, at times has been influenced by political changes.

Table 8.7

University and Degree College Teachers' Interest in Politics

Interest	*University Level* Number	%	*College Level* Number	%	*Total*	%
Intense	80	53.3	75	50.0	155	51.7
Mild	60	40.0	50	33.3	110	36.7
Nil	10	6.7	25	16.7	35	11.6
Total	150	100	150	100	300	100

The present data confirms this fact that overwhelming majority of teachers have political interest. As table 8.7 shows that 51.7% teachers were intensely interested in the politics, while 36.7% teachers were mildly interested and 11.7% teachers not nil interested in the politics.

TEACHERS' FAMILIES POLITICAL COMPLEXION

The family, it has been stated earlier, plays a vital role in one's socialization. Now socialization also implies politicization[6], for some of the values, inculcated through socialization are manifestly political while others have political implications or overtones. Robert Lane[7] suggest three ways in which family play its politicizing role:

(i) Overt and covert indoctrination
(ii) Putting the child in a particular social context (shall we say class position?), and,
(iii) Moulding the child's personality.

These, says Lane, constitute the *"Mendelian Law of Politics"*.

It is not necessary to discuss these or other ways in which family politicize the individual. The thing to be noted in that of the various or factors of family, its political complexion is particularly in the context of the development and study of teacher's political background.

Table 8.8

Interest in Politics of University and Degree College Teachers' Parents

	University Level		*College Level*		*Total*	*%*
Interest	*Number*	*%*	*Number*	*%*		
Intense	30	20	35	23.3	65	21.7
Mild	38	25.3	40	26.7	78	26.0
Nil	68	54.7	75	50.0	143	52.3

As table 8.8 reveals that 52.3% were not interested in the politics and 47.7% teachers' parents had political interest.

Table 8.9

Political Workers in University and Degree College Teachers' Family

	University Level		*College Level*		*Total*	*%*
Political Workers	*Number*	*%*	*Number*	*%*		
Yes	52	34.7	38	25.3	90	30
No	98	65.3	112	74.7	210	70
Total	150	100	150	100	300	100

Table 8.9 exhibits that most teachers did not have any political workers in their families and 30% teachers had political workers in the family.

REASON FOR REJECTING POLITICAL PARTY

It has been pointed out that most activists in the west do not join the political parties chiefly because of the latter's bureaucratic functioning and political opportunism.

Table 8.10

University and Degree College Teachers Reason for Rejecting the Political Party

Reasons	*University Level* Number	%	*College Level* Number	%	*Total*	%
(i) Not Proper During Teaching	50	33.3	30	20	80	26.7
(ii) To Retain Personal Freedom	15	10.0	10	6.7	25	8.3
(iii) Opportunism of Political Parties	8	5.3	15	10	23	7.7
(iv) Due to Govt. Service	30	20.0	18	12	48	16.0
(v) Family Objection	25	16.7	15	10	40	13.3
(vi) No Specific Reason	22	14.7	62	41.3	84	28.0
Total	150	100	150	100	300	100

Table 8.10 shows that 26.7% teachers did not join the political party due to their teaching profession, 8.3% said that they retain their personal freedom so they did not join the political parties, 7.6% teachers did not join politics due to opportunism of political parties, 16% teachers due to government jobs did not joined the political parties, 13.3% teachers family objection were the factor of rejecting the parties and 28% teachers did not have any specific reason for rejecting the political parties.

LEVEL OF INTEREST

Politics have covered entire social life tightly. Nobody can escape from politics. People take interest or get involve in politics in one way or other.

Table 8.11

Level of Interest in Politics of the University and Degree College Teachers

Type of Politics	*University Level* Number	%	*College Level* Number	%	*Total*	%
International	10	8.3	25	20	35	14.2
National	80	66.7	45	36	125	51.0
Local	10	8.3	35	28	45	18.4
Only Professional Level	20	16.7	20	16	40	16.4
Total	120	100	125	100	1245	100

The above table reveals that 14.2% teachers take part in international politics, 51% take part in national politics, 18.4% take part in local politics and, 16.4% teachers take part in professional level politics.

OPINION REGARDING COMMUNAL RIOTS AND COMMUNALISM

Communalism has been the worst type of disaster. It has put to loss human society for ages. Communalism has been a incurable disease spreading over the entire Earth. It is as old as the religion itself. First crime which was committed on this Earth regarding communalism was on the son of Adam, first great son *Prophet* on this Earth killed his real brother, another son of Adam. Since then unaccountable number of human beings have slaughtered in many countries of the world. Even today their has been communal killings and communal tension allover the world. Recently in India there had been riots and communal murders. Communal tension has not totally vanished and every moment inhabitants are facing threats to their lives and property.

The phenomenon of communalism is an extremely complex one and is generally associated with plural societies. While in the West Communalism is used to mean a feeling and a concern for the Community in India the term has a negative connotation. The over concern with one's community is reflected in an antagonistic feeling towards other communities. When people of other communities within their own society they are supposed to inflame communal feelings. Scholars have given different definitions of this phenomenon. Some of them defined the term communalism as an outgrowth of religious and cultural differences between the Hindus and the Muslims. These differences have created antagonism and distrust between them. Thus Khan regards communalism "as a form of indifference, condescension, hatred, and aggressive attitude towards all the members of the religious community that one's own based on a real or imaginary threat from and individual or a group of that community".[8]

Humayun Kabir explains Communalism as a minority versus majority problem in a plural and democratic society. He is of the view that democracy is a necessary precondition for the emergence of minority problem.[9]

The noted historian, Bipin Chandra has been more specific in characterizing communalism. According to him, communalism occurs when the following three conditions are fulfilled—

1. People who follow the same religions have common secular interest.
2. When secular interests of different religions are dissimilar or divergent from the followers of other religion, and
3. When interests of different religions are sent to be incompatible, antagonistic and hostile.[10]

According to Pramod Kumar "Communalism does not protect the interest of one religious group at the cost of other and it does not benefit the community in whose name it seeks concessions but may only benefit a few individuals with in that community."[11]

The Marxist scholar Randhir Singh regards communalism above all, "as aspect of politics of the ruling classes in a Society with a massive feudal colonial inheritance, deep "religious divisions and undergoing its own historically specific form of capitalist development."[12]

Pradeep Nayak defines communalism as a political mobilization on the basis of religious identity of a community by the political elite to serve their interest in maintaining political power. In his view communalism should be perceived as a State mobilization of a community for a political purpose to form a political community out of religious issues.[13]

In the light of these definitions, following features of communalism can be chalked out —

1. Communalism is associated with religious affiliation.
2. It unites people of a particular religious faith for secular causes and thus uses religion for political purposes.
3. It arises from a perceived or even concocted threat from the other religious group.
4. It creates greater-in-group solidarity by creating negative stereotype about the out group.
5. Communalism expresses itself in violent tensions designed to hurt the other party-riots, arson and even attack on the religious faith of other party.
6. It also derives support from the follower of same faith but belonging to other political factions.

Respondents were asked to give their opinion about communalism. As expected most teachers discard communalism usually who are literate educated persons provoke people inspire them and make them fight communal war. Such respondents who discarded communal riots constituted 95.3%, while those opined in favour of communalism were only 4.7%. This communal opinion shows teachers' conservative background and hence we can mention here percentage of these type of teachers are less but some conservative and though minded teachers are present in our educational setup, so they can influence their pupils and their personality.

Table 8.12

Opinion Regarding Communal Riots of University and Degree College Teachers

Opinion	*University Level*		*College Level*		*Total*	*%*
	Number	*%*	*Number*	*%*		
Discard Communal Riots	142	94.7	144	96	286	95.3
Accept Communal Riots	8	5.3	6	4	14	4.7
Total	150	100	150	100	300	100

Communalism is such an act of hatred which cannot be pardoned, therefore nobody takes its responsibility. People from different groups, organizational, political parties and gundas are responsible for communal riots and tensions. They have their own vested interest. They create tension and impose responsibility on one another.

Table 8.13

Evaluation of Responsibility of Communal Riots by University and Degree College Teachers

Evaluation	*University Level*		*College Level*		*Total*	*%*
	Number	*%*	*Number*	*%*		
Religious Person	85	56.6	75	50	160	53.3
Political Person	40	26.7	55	26.7	95	31.7
Masses	25	16.7	20	13.3	45	15.0
Total	150	100	150	100	300	100

Data regarding responsibility of communalism exhibit that 53.3% teachers treated religious personalities responsible for communalism. Political person has been thought, equally responsible for communalism by 31.7% and 15% teachers fixed responsibility on gundas for spreading communalism.

MANDIR-MASJID ISSUE

On 6th December, 1992 the Babri Mosque was demolished by the uncontrolled crowd that had assembled from all parts of India. To be sure, the demolition was never stated as part of the agenda of those who organized the congregation for the Kar Seva.

The whole country was shocked and surprised at receiving the news of the demolition of the disputed structure. The print media, electric media and every thinking man condemned this act. The then Prime Minister P.V. Narismha Rao said, "I have been betrayed by the BJP." On 7 December 1992, the Supreme Court, during an emergency hearing on an application seeking the appointment of the centre as a receiver of disputed property, said that, "it is great pity that a constitutionally elected government could not discharge its sensitive duties in a matter of this magnitude. This is the first time that an assurance by the State Government that it will protect the structure and carry out the court orders has been violated." Expressing great concern over the repercussion of the county K.K. Venugopal, the Senior Counsel for the State Government agreed with the Judges and said, "the repercussions were mind-boggling for the future of the country. I had my head in shame for what has happened."[1]

The controversy over Ramjanam Bhoomi versus Babri Masjid is no doubt one of the most sensitive and emotional issues which polarized the Hindus and Muslims in India.

Mandir-Masjid issue is also a part of conservatism. Conservatism is provoked on the basis of certain conservative man made issue. That issue is propagated on large scale.

Religious feelings are exploited to a great extent. Then with one appropriate stroke rioting is made to burst and it wraps the entire society.

The respondents were interviewed regarding Mandir-Masjid issue. They were directly asked about the issue. The respondents told that it is not in the interest of the country when they are asked whether the issue was in the interest of the country. Those radical teachers who found the issue against the interest of the country were 78.3%. There were 53 such teachers who said that the issue was in the interest of the Hindus. Percentage of such teachers was 17.7%. Whether it was in the interest of the Muslims 4% of the respondents replied affirmative, that it was in the interest of the Muslims.

Table 8.14
University and Degree College Teachers Reaction regarding Mandir-Masjid Issues

Reaction of the Issues	*University Level Number*	*%*	*College Level Number*	*%*	*Total*	*%*
It is not in the Interest of Country	120	180.0	115	76.7	235	78.3
It is in the Interest of Hindu	25	16.7	28	18.7	53	17.7
It is in the Interest	5	3.3	7	4.6	12	4.0
Total	150	100	150	100	300	150

Mandir-Masjid issue has assumed bigger shape. It is now total India's issue. Not only Indians but peoples residing in different foreign countries have concerned with this issue. The Mandir-Masjid issue have put up masses and their property to a great loss. Everybody wished to find out a solution. Many of us try to chalk out headlines of a solution.

Table 8.15
University and Degree College Teachers' Faith regarding Solution of the Issue

Faith of Issue	*University Level* Number	%	*College Level* Number	%	*Total*	%
People should wait for the decision of the court	25	16.7	30	20.0	55	18.3
Should sit together and decide	20	13.3	20	13.3	40	13.3
Government should take stern action	105	70.0	100	66.7	205	68.4
Total	150	100	150	100	300	100

A thorough analysis of the data available lays down that 55 respondents constituting 18.3% opined that people should wait for court's design. There were 13.6% such respondents who have to say that Hindus and Muslims should sit together and seek some remedy of the disease. Most of the respondents on the question of solution of the issue said that government should take over the issue and take action and reach a decision. Most of the respondents (68.4%) gave their opinion in this issue on its favour.

MAJOR PROBLEMS OF THE COUNTRY

Developing countries have multidimensional problems. They have to struggle to overcome those problems. It seems that problems and development position of a country have reciprocal relations. Plenty of problems for country to enlist itself among developed society in other words they stopped the country to develop and it may also be taken into consideration it is the developing nature of the country which does not enable a country to develop and specially. India has been a developing country and there has been abundance of problems. Such endless type of problems can be traced in India which presses only to laugh at them. But lot of money and manpower and force is invested to solve or to control those problems.

Table 8.16

Major Problems of the Country Assessed by University and Degree College Teachers

Problems of the Country	*University Level* Number	%	*College Level* Number	%	*Total*	%
Unemployment	60	140.0	65	43.3	125	41.7
Terrorism	30	20	25	16.7	55	18.3
Corruption in Govt. Department	20	13.3	20	13.3	40	13.3
Leadership in India	28	18.7	15	10.0	43	14.3
Religious Problem	12	8.0	25	16.7	37	12.4
Total	150	100	150	100	300	100

Facts concerning different problems were collected during survey. Respondents told that they thought that unemployment as the most serious problem. Those who said so were 41.7%. Terrorism is another serious problem as 18.3% respondents said. Corruption in the country was a serious problem as 13.3% opined. Those who are to lead the country in the right direction became problem and created problems as 14.3% respondents told. Religion which to fetch salvation to the people raises a problem as it has done so now in the country. 12.4% teachers said that religious problem was the serious problem.

MEASURES TAKEN BY THE GOVERNMENT

Government always tries to solve the problems. If is moves in right direction the problem is solved. Sometimes in democratic system party interested is served first and the problems are neglected. Most frequently ruling party finds its interest fulfilled, then it tries to solve the problem. And it is sees that party's interest requires to keep the problem alive, it buries the issue and neglects it. These comes such stages in the life span of a country that all the governmental machinery stands weaker than the strength of problem as the problem of terrorism in India.

Table 8.17

Satisfaction of the University and Degree College Teachers with the Measures Taken by the Government

Satisfaction of Teachers	*University Level* Number	*University Level* %	*College Level* Number	*College Level* %	*Total*	*%*
Satisfied	90	60.0	78	52	168	56
Not satisfied	60	40.0	72	48	132	44
Total	150	100	150	100	300	100

Respondents were asked to tell whether measures to solve the burning problems of the country were sufficient. This question was replied by 56% in affirmative and 44% in negative.

IDEOLOGICAL ORIENTATIONS

Ideology, declares Daniel Bell[14] is dead in the affluent (capitalist) countries of the west. It has died of two things: (i) the alleged embourgeoisement of the working class resulting from its new-found affluence, and (ii) convergence of industrial societies[15] (both capitalist and socialist), which has produced a "post–industrial society" in which the decisions are no longer political, but managerial and technical. Further, both these developments are said to have refuted Marx's thesis on capitalist development; and "the end of ideology", says Harrington, is a shorthand way of saying the end of socialism..."[16]. For Bell's argument is that socialism, which arose to demystify the capitalist ideology, has itself become an ideology and irrelevant.

This much publicized end of ideology (that is, end of "economic radicalism" and political extremism) thesis has, however, been disputed on the following counts.

First, embourgeoisement is "disproved in the streets" by the huge waves of workers' strikes which have recently been sweeping the highly developed countries like the US[17], Britain, France and Germany. Second, the equivalence of life style has not resulted in status equivalence (as shown in endogamy and social mixing) of middle and working classes. Third, the workers' affluence itself turns out to be a illusory if viewed (as it must be not in absolute but relative terms—relative to (i) capitalists "profits" (which have increased at a higher and faster rate than workers wages) and middle class economic security and fringe benefits etc., and (ii) the cost of living.[18] Fourth, trade unionism is particularly strong among the better paid workers, which suggest that affluence as such is hardly a guarantee against militancy. This is not to deny the existence of what Lenin calls "Labour aristocracy" corrupted by capitalism, but the point is that this labour aristocracy has failed to subdue or stamp out workers' struggle. Finally, as for the end of ideology refuting Karl Marx, the propounders of this thesis have got their Marx wrong. Firstly, Marx's prediction about the increasing misery or improverishment of the workers under capitalism does not refer to their material conditions but to their dehumanization and alienation, which have surely deepened with the growth of monopoly capitalism. The standard of living, the critics point out has undoubtedly gone up in the affluent capitalist countries like America, but the quality of life has deteriorated. As Reich puts it: "Of all the forms of impoverishment that can be seen or felt in America, loss of self or death in life, is surely the most devasting".[19] Secondly, it is un-Marxian to regard the workers as bourgeois just because they so regard or define themselves, for Marxism is opposed to treating consciousness as the basic defining criterion of class.

The Marxist critics, chiefly of the "old" Left, therefore, reject the end of ideology thesis as bourgeois propaganda stuff. The end of ideology, they say, is itself the ideology of the *status quo* in the sense that if the so-called good society has already been established, then by definition, the need for what C. Wright Mills calls "structural criticism" no longer obtains. Similarly, convergence is also seen as open to question; and Alvin Gouldner has this to say about the contention that decisions in the so-called post industrial society are no more political but technical. "To limit judgement solely to autonomous' technical criteria is in effect not only to allow but to require men to be moral cretins in their technical roles."[20]

Indian history shows that there was never any ideological orientation except Mahatma Gandhi's ideology, but that ideology was limited only for the freedom struggle. In Indian history we find only social thinkers and reformers like Dayanand Saraswati, Vivekanand and Aurbindo Ghosh etc. But all of them have no active orientations, to change the entire Indian society.

Now ideology may or may not be dead in the affluent Westorn countries, but it certainly is a vital force in the Asian, African and Latin American Countries. In India, the credit for giving an ideological orientation to as thinking largely goes to Jawahar Lal Nehru. As Independent India's first Prime Minister, he proclaimed *"the socialistic pattern of society"* as the national goal and greatly popularized the idea of socialism. But after his death, a section of political leadership made strong attempts to de-ideologise our policies and thinking. Thus it did by stressing that our economic development was not an ideological issues and by demanding a *"pragmatic"* approach to the country's problem. In fact, Jawahar Lal Nehru's successor, Lal Bahadur Shastri himself took this line, and almost completely dropped the world socialism from his policy statements and public speeches. It is however, obvious that the so-called pragmatic approach was really a subtle denigration of India's leftward orientation and implied a rightist swing. After her father's death Mrs. Indira Gandhi also advocated pragmatism in the beginning, but circumstances soon forced her to restore her father, Jawahar Lal Nehru's ideological orientation in public issues. In fact, she has been chiefly responsible for growing ideological polarization orientation in the country. After the tragic assassination of Mrs. Indira Gandhi, Mr. Rajeev Gandhi held the reins of the country. He with his vision of youth endeavoured to take a strong India into the 21st century and encouraged the youth of the country to take on active part in this exercise.

During the time of V.P. Singh Mandal Commission recommendations regarding the provision of reservation ignited caste conflicts in the country. All the policies of Prime Minister P.V. Narasimha Rao are based on the democratic secular pattern. He has tried to establish new industries with foreign collaboration and generate employment for the country's youth as well as develop the technology in the country.

In the contemporary Indian society there have been a growth of many problems like Mandir-Masjid issue, Punjab and Kashmir terrorism, Casteism, cross border terrorism, unemployment education, slum area, population, explosion, women problem, poor health problems etc. For realizing the dream of a democratic secular India the government would have to find solution for the above problems. Otherwise in future these problems may become more dangerous and damaging.

It was therefore nothing surprising that most of the teachers (83.3%) had ideologically oriented while 16.7% teachers were uncommitted. The percentage of rightist was 48.3% and 35% were leftist.

Table 8.18

University and Degree College Teachers' Ideological Orientation

Ideology	*University Level* *Number*	*%*	*College Level* *Number*	*%*	*Total*	*%*
Rightist	70	46.5	75	50	145	48.3
Leftist	50	33.3	55	36.7	105	35.0
Uncommitted	30	20.0	20	13.3	50	16.7
Total	150	100	150	100	300	100

FINDINGS

A study of activism and politicization of respondents show that only 15% teachers participated in activism at school, college, university and professional levels. Investigations revealed that 9.3% teachers were gone on hunger strike before and after joining the university. Respondents told that 3.7% gone once a time on hunger strike, 2.3% two times, 2% have gone three times and 1.3% teachers were gone on hunger strike more than three times. A maximum percentage (90.7) were never gone on hunger strike. On the question of election contest at any state only 9.3 per cent teachers of university and college level have contested the election. In which most teachers 6 per cent were contested only time, 2 per cent two times and 1 per cent have contested the election more than three times. Data regarding the arrest record of police shows that 15.6 per cent teachers have a police arrest record before joining the university and 6.7 per cent were arrested after joining the university. Analysis of socio-cultural activities of university and college teachers shows that 65.7 per cent teachers have more participated in socio-cultural activities and 20 per cent have participated in it mildly, only 14.3 per cent teachers have never attended the socio-cultural activities. The detailed analysis of teachers' interest in politics shows that 88.4 per cent (51.7%) interestingly and 36.7% mildly interested) teachers were interested in the politics.

Only 11.6 per cent teachers were not interested in politics. In investigation regarding the family political background of teachers shows that 52.3 per cent teachers' parents were intensely and mildly interested in politics while 70 per cent teachers were not having any political leader or worker in their families and only 30 per cent teachers from university and associated college teachers were having a political leader in their families. Investigations regarding the rejecting political parties the respondents told that they reject the party due to their teaching profession, 26.7 per cent teachers said it, 8.3 percent teachers told that due to return the personal freedom, 7.7 per cent teachers reject the politics due to the opportunism of political parties, 16 percent were not joining the party due to their government service, 13.3 per cent teachers' family members were not in favour of political participation and 28 per cent teachers had no specific reason for rejecting the political parties. Investigation regarding the interest of politics 51% teachers were interested in the national level politics. Respondents told that 95.3% did not like communal riots. On the question of fixing responsibility of communal riots, 53.7% opined that it was religious process who motivated people to fight and 31.7% treated political process responsible for communal tensions, and 15% teachers told that masses were responsible for the communal riots. Regarding Mandir-Masjid issue most of the teachers (78.3%) said that it was not in the interest of the country. Investigations revealed that 68.4% teachers wished that government showed stern action to solve the Mandir-Masjid issue. According to most of the teachers (41.7%) the biggest problem was unemployment. Government should try to solve these problems, 56% felt satisfied regarding steps taken, 44% were not satisfied with the efforts done by the government. Most of the teachers were ideologically oriented (83.3%) and 16.7% were uncommitted. The percentage of rightist was 48.3% and leftist was 35 per cent.

REFERENCES

1. Max Weber, *The Theory of Social and Economic Organization*, trans., A.M. Henderson and Talcott Parsons (New York: Oxford University Press, 1946).
2. Hans Gerth and C. Writh Mills, *From Max Weber: Essays in Sociology* (New York: Oxford University Press, 1946.
3. Gerth and Mills, *op. cit*.
4. James McKee, Sociology: *The Study of Society*, CBS, College Publishing, Holt Rinehart and Winston, 1974.
5. Lister W. Milbrath, *Political Participation: How and why People get involved in Politic*, (Chicago: Rand McNally, 1965).
6. Laswell and Abraham Kaplan, *Power and Society*, New Haven (Yale Paperback), 1950, p. 145.
7. Robert Lane, : "Fathers and Sons : The Foundations of Political Beliefs" *American Journal of Society* 24, 1959, 0. 502-511.
8. M. Rafiq Khan, *Forms of Communalism, National Integration : Its meaning and Relevance*, Navchetan Prakashan, Varanasi, 1970. p. 201.
9. Humayun Kabir, *Minorities in a Democracy*, K.L. Mukhopadhay, Calcutta, 1968.
10. Bipin Chandra, *Communalism in Modern India*, Vikas Publishing House, New Delhi, 1987.
11. Pramod Kumar, *Polluting Sacred Faith: A Study of Communalism and Violence*, Ajanta Publications, Delhi, 1992.
12. Randhir Singh, - "Communalism and the Struggle Against Communalism: A Marxist View", as Cited in K.N. Panikar (ed.) *Communalism in Indian History, Politics and Culture*. Manohar Publications, Delhi, 1991.
13. Pradeep Nayak, *The Politics of Ayodhya Dispute: Rise of Communalism and Future Voting Behaviour*, Commonwealth Publishers, New Delhi.
14. Daniell Bell, *The End of Ideology*, Glencoe, 1960. Seymour Martin Lipset, *Political Man*, 1960.
15. Ian Wenberg, "The Problem of the Convergence of Industrial Societies: A critical look at the State of Theory", *Comparative Studies in Society and History*, Vol. II, No. 1, January 1969, pp 103-104.

16. Michael Harrington, *The Accidental Century*, Penguine Book,s 1967, pp 103-104
17. A Valyuzhenich, "A close-up of the Affluent Soceity" *New Times*, No. 40, October 17, 1970 and Herbert Marcuse, *One Dimensional Man*, 1959.
18. Charles, A. Reich, *The Greening of America*, New York, 1970.
19. Stephen, W. Roussens and James Farganis, "American" Politics and the End of Ideology, in Irving Louis Horowtiz (ed), *The New Sociology*, New York, 1964.
20. Alvin W. Gouldner, *The Coming Crisis of Western Sociology*, p. 13.

Chapter 9

Teachers' Attitude Towards Radicalism and Conservatism

As man in his finite world is repeatedly forced to cope with the same object, the repeatedly evoked cognitions, feelings and response dispositions become organized into a united and enduring system-for man is an organizing and conserving animal. This entire package" of particular beliefs, feelings and responses tendencies is henceforth always there, on the ready, whenever the individual is confronted by the appropriate object. In other words he now has an attitude toward the object.

And as the individual acquire more and more attitudes–as he "assimilates" more and more objects in his world—his improvisations towards these objects and his fresh examinations and interpretations of them decrease. His actions become conservative, predictable and consistent—and social life become possible. For where these are no enduring beliefs, evaluations and action tendencies, which can be shared by a company of men, social life as we know it would be impossible.

Attitudes are broadly viewed as specific response to particular objects. These responses determine the likes and dislikes and the differential values which a person attaches to different objects or phenomenon. Attitudes are an indicator of a future act. It is thus significant in regulating the behaviour patterns of the individual. The development of attitudes is, therefore, directly related to learning and experience. Man always strives to understand the physical and social attitudes which surround him.

Usually persons have internally consistent, overall attitudes. It is a reflection of their generality of attitudes. Some people can be labelled as radicals or conservatives because they have consistent attitudes towards a wide range of objects, such as religion, education etc., knowing whether a person is a radical or conservative, fairly accurate predictions can be made about his attitudes towards a wide variety of issue. Now the question arises as to whether a person who is conservative in one area of life will be conservative in other areas too or not?

Many authors like Dewey (1922), Allport (1929), Vetter (1930-31), Alport and Sargent (1941), and Saneis (1952) found considerable generality and internal consistency in radicalism conservatism.

Bogardus (1931), too strongly believes in specificity of attitudes and says "Attitudes are as numerous as the objects to which a person responds".

Some another theorist (Katz and Stotland, 1959, Rejeck; 1982, Triandis, 1971) have purposed that attitudes have three components: affect, behavioural tendencies and cognition (the ABC component model of attitudes). The affective component describes one's emotional reaction toward the attitude object, the behavioural component includes the behaviour associated with the attitude object and the cognitive component includes beliefs, facts and information about the object.

There are several basic characteristics of attitudes. First, attitudes are inferred from the way individuals behave, which could include the behaviour of filling out an attitude questionnaire. Second, attitudes are directed toward a psychological object or category. People categorise in different ways'. One's own conceptual system determines how one categorizes the object toward which attitudes are directed. Third attitudes are learned. Because attitudes are learned, it follows that they can be changed. Finally, attitudes influence behaviours. Holding an attitude toward an object gives one a reason to have toward the object in a certain way.

To analyse the attitude of male and female, university and its degree college teachers towards radicalism and conservatism in three areas of life namely personal, social, and religious. The objective III is framed to visualize the attitude of the whole sample towards radicalism and conservatism. A five point scale is used for scoring the attitude of Lucknow University and its associated degree college teachers. There were 60 items in the questionnaire based on L.N. Dubey radical-conservative attitude scale, and the scale have been classified into five categories. L.N. Dubey has given the range of scores in the manual, the maximum score for highly radical 300, 240 for radical, 180 for moderate, 120 for conservative and 60 for highly conservative for an individual.

Table 9.1

Attitude of the Whole Sample Towards Radicalism and Conservatism

Category	*Class Interval*	*Frequency*	*%*
Highly Radical	240 and above	110	36.6
Radical	200-239	110	36.6
Moderate	160-199	50	16.6
Conservative	140-159	13	4.3
Highly Conservative	139 and below	17	5.6
Total		N = 300	

Table 9.1 shows the attitude of the whole sample towards radicalism and conservatism in the following manner.

The data collected shows that 36.6% teachers are in the category of highly radicals and 36.6% are also in the category of radicals. 16.6% teachers are in the category of moderates, 4.3% teachers are in the category of conservatives and 5.6% teachers are in the category of highly conservatives. Hence few teachers are conservative and highly conservative, most of them are highly radical, and modern.

(1) to Analyze the attitude of the Two Respective Groups

The sample of the study for the objective third is categorized into two categories viz. male teachers and female teachers, group consisting equal number of teachers from two groups, one group is from University of Lucknow and second group from its associated degree college level, 150 teachers (97 male teachers and 53 female teaches) from Lucknow University level and 150 teachers C80 male teachers and 70 female teachers) from associated degree college were taken for the study. The following data of two respective groups obtained.

Table 9.2

Showing Mean Difference Between Attitudes of Male and Female Teachers

Group of Respondents	*Numbers*	*Mean*	*Standard Deviation*	*Value of 't'*	*Conclusion*
Male	177	220.5	12.4	0.25	Not Significant at 0.05 Level.
Female	123	214.5	13.35		
Total	300-2=298				

In table 9.2 the value of 't' i.e., the difference between two mean is 0.25 and 298 (177 + 123 - 2 = 298) degree of freedom the calculated value is 1.92 on 0.05 level of significance which means the difference is not significant at 0.05 and 0.01 level.

Hence, the Ho (null hypothesis) is retained at 0.05 level and 0.01 level of significance.

(2) To analyze the attitude of two male teachers from University and its Associated Degree Colleges with reference to Personal, Social and Religious areas of Life-

The sample of the present study was categorized into two groups. And the following data of two respective group obtained.

Table 9.3

Mean Difference between Lucknow University and its Associated Degree College Male Teachers Attitude Towards Radicalism and Conservatism

Group of Respondents	*Numbers*	*Mean*	*Standard Deviation*	*Value of 't'*	*Conclusion*
Lucknow University Males	97	221.7	13.98	0.64	Not Significant at 0.05 Level.
Associated Degree Colleges Male	80	216.6	25.21		
Total	177				

In Table 9.3 the value of 't' i.e. the difference between two mean is 0.64 and at 175 (97 + 80 - 2 =175) degree of freedom the calculated value is 1.97 on 0.05 level of significance which means the difference is not significant at 0.05 level and 0.01 level. Hence the Ho (null hypothesis) is retained at 0.05 level.

(3) To analyze the attitude of female teachers from Lucknow University and its Associated Degree Colleges with reference to their social personal and religious areas of Life-

The sample of the present study was categorized into two groups, and the following data of two respective groups obtained.

Table 9.4

Mean Difference of Female Teachers from Lucknow University and its Associated Degree College Towards Radicalism and Conservatism

Group of Respondents	*Numbers*	*Mean*	*Standard Deviation*	*Value of 't'*	*Conclusion*
Lucknow University Males	53	223.8	30.65	0.17	Not Significant at 0.05 Level
Associated Degree Colleges Male	70	224.6	15.10		
Total	123				

In Table 9.4 the value of 't' i.e. the difference between two mean is 0.17 and at 121 (53 + 70 - 2 =121) degree of freedom the calculated value is 1.98 on 0.05 level of significance which means the difference is not significant at 0.05 level and 0.01 level.

Hence the Ho (null hypothesis) is retained at 0.05 level.

(4) To analyze the attitude of Lucknow University male teachers and Degree Colleges female teachers attitude with reference to their personal, social and religious areas of Life-

The sample of the present study was categorized into two groups, and the following data of respective groups obtained.

In Table 9.5 the value of 't' i.e. the difference between two mean is 2, and at 165 (97 + 70 - 2 =165) degree of freedom the calculated value is 1.98 on 0.05 level of significance which means the difference is not significant at 0.05 level.

Hence the Ho (null hypothesis) is retained at 0.05 level.

Table 9.5

Mean Difference of Male Teachers from University Level and Female Teachers from Associated Degree College Towards Radicalism and Conservatism

Group of Respondents	*Numbers*	*Mean*	*Standard Deviation*	*Value of 't'*	*Conclusion*
University Males Teachers	97	221.7	13.98	2	Significant at 0.05 Level.
Degree Colleges Female Teachers	70	224.6	15.10		
Total	167				

(5) To analyze the attitude of Male and Female Teachers from University level and associated Degree Colleges level with respect to their social personal and religious areas of life.

The sample of the present study was categorized into two groups, male and female teachers. The following data of two respective groups were obtained.

Table 9.6

Mean Difference of Lucknow University Male and Female Teachers Attitude Towards Radicalism and Conservatism

Group of Respondents	*Numbers*	*Mean*	*Standard Deviation*	*Value of 't'*	*Conclusion*
Male Teachers of Lucknow University	97	221.7	13.98	0.53	Not Significant at 0.05 Level.
Female Teachers of Lucknow University	53	223.8	30.65		
Total	150				

In Table 9.6 the value of 't' i.e. the difference between two mean is 0.53, and at 148 (97 + 53 - 2 =148) degree of freedom the calculated value is 1.98 on 0.05 level of significant at 0.05 level.

Hence the Ho (null hypothesis) is retained at 0.05 level.

(6) To analyze the attitude of Male and Female Teachers of Lucknow University and Associated Degree Colleges level with respect to their social personal and religious areas of life.

The sample of the present study was categorized into two groups and the following data of two respective groups obtained.

Table 9.7

Mean Difference of Male and Female Degree College Teachers Attitude Towards Radicalism and Conservatism

Group of Respondents	*Numbers*	*Mean Deviation*	*Standard*	*Value of 't'*	*Conclusion*
Degree College Male Teachers	80	216.6	25.21	3.7	Significant at 0.05 Level.
Degree Colleges Female Teachers	70	224.6	15.10		
Total	150				

In Table 9.7 the difference between two mean in 3.7, and at 148 (80 + 70 - 2 =148) degree of freedom the calculated value is 1.98 on 0.05 level of significance which means the difference is significant at 0.05 level and 0.01 level.

Hence the Ho (null hypothesis) is rejected at 0.05 level.

(7) To find out the relationship between age and attitude of Male and Female Teachers towards radicalism and conservatism in three areas of life, namely personal social and religious.

The sample is categorized into two categories i.e. above 40 years and below 40 years male and female teachers. Following data of two respective groups were obtained.

Table 9.8

Mean Difference between Attitudes of 40 years above and 40 years below male and female teachers of Lucknow University and its Associated Degree Colleges

Age Group	*Numbers*	*Mean*	*Standard Deviation*	*Value of 't'*	*Conclusion*
Above 40 years	M	90	224.5	15.6 1.57	Not Significant at 0.05 Level
Above 40 years	F	70	222.6	28.6	
40 years and below	M	87	218.5	26.1 0.38	Not Significant at 0.05 Level
40 years and below	F	53	223.7	14.1	
Total		300			

In the Table 9.8 the value of first 't' i.e. the difference between two mean (above 40 years male and female Lucknow University and its associated degree college teachers) is 1.57 which is not significant at either level.

The second value of 't' i.e. the difference between two mean (40 years and below male and female teachers of Lucknow University and its associated degree college) is 0.38 which is not significant at .05 level and. 01 level of significance.

Hence the Ho (null hypothesis) is retained at .05 level and .01 level of significance.

(8) To analyze the attitude of two respective qualified groups of male and female teachers from Lucknow University and its Associated Degree Colleges

The sample is categorized into two groups viz., above post graduate (Ph.D., D.Litt., Diploma), male and female teachers, and only post graduate male and female teachers. In the first group there were 130 male teachers and 70 female teachers were presented and in only post graduate group there were 87 male teachers and 53 female teachers were present following data of two respective group obtained.

Table 9.9

Mean Difference between attitudes of above and only Post Graduate Male and Female Teachers of Lucknow University and its Associated Degree Colleges.

Age Group	*Numbers*	*Mean*	*Standard Deviation*	*Value of 't'*	*Conclusion*
Above Post Graduate	M	130	100.5	8.81 0.02	Not Significant
Above Post Graduate	F	100	90.5	9.47	at 0.05 Level
Only Post Graduate	M	47	78.5	6.70 0.04	Not Significant
Only Post Graduate	F	23	75.5	7.23	at 0.05 Level
Total		300			

In Table 9.9 the value of first 't' i.e. the difference between two mean (above post graduate level male and female teachers of Lucknow University and its associated degree colleges) is 0.02, which is not significant at 0.05 and 0.91 level of significance.

The value of second 't' i.e. the difference between two mean (post graduate level only) is 0.04 which is not significant at either level.

Hence the Ho (null hypothesis) is retained at 0.05 and 0.01 level of significance.

(9) To analyze the attitude of male and female teachers Lucknow University and its Associated Degree Colleges in personal area of life-

The sample was categorized into two groups male and female consisting equal numbers. Following data of two respective group obtained.

Table 9.10

Means Difference between University and its Associated Degree College (M/F) Teachers Attitude Towards Radicalism and Conservatism in their Personal Area of Life

Group of Respondents	*Numbers*	*Mean*	*Standard Deviation*	*Value of 't'*	*Conclusion*
Male	150	79.6	18.38	0.73	Not Significant at either level
Female	150	81.7	8.54		
Total	300				

In Table 9.10 the value of 't' i.e. the difference between two mean is 0.73 which is not significant at either level.

Hence Ho (null hypothesis) is retained at 0.05 and 0.01 level of significance.

(10) To analyze the attitude of male and female teachers from Lucknow University and its Associated Degree Colleges in social area of life.

The sample was categorized into two groups male and female consisting equal numbers. Following data of two respective group were obtained.

Table 9.11

Mean Difference between University and its Associated Degree College (M/F) Teachers' Attitude in their Social Area of Life

Group of Respondents	*Numbers*	*Mean*	*Standard Deviation*	*Value of 't'*	*Conclusion*
Male	150	78.4	8.81	0.95	Not Significant at either level
Female	150	81.9	9.47		
Total	300				

In Table 9.11 the value of 't' i.e. the difference between two mean in 0.95 which is not significant difference in male and female teacher's attitude towards conservatism and radicalism in social area of life.

Hence the Ho (null hypothesis) is retained at 0.05 and 0.01 level of significance.

(11) To analyze the attitude of male and female teachers from Lucknow University and its Associated Degree College teachers in the religious area of life.

The present sample was categorized into two groups (male and female). Following data of two respective group were obtained.

Table 9.12

Mean Difference between University and Associated Degree College Male and Female Teachers Attitude in Religious area of Life

Group of Respondents	*Numbers*	*Mean*	*Standard Deviation*	*Value of 't'*	*Conclusion*
Male	150	79.1	11.27	0.41	Not Significant at either level
Female	150	81.1	8.83		
Total	300				

In Table 9.12 the value of 6.12 the value of 't' i.e. the difference between two mean is 0.41 which is not significant at 0.05 and 0.01 level of significance.

Hence Ho (null hypothesis) is retained at .05 and .01 level of significance.

FINDINGS

On the basis of above findings, it is clear that most teachers are highly radical and radical but very few teachers are conservative and highly conservative. Young people are more dynamic and more adaptable, more progressive and are not tough minded they do accept social change easily. It is found that it does not matter whether they are males or females.

The data that there is no significant difference between male and female teachers attitude on the basis of their sex.

As the study is conducted for the Lucknow University and its associated degree colleges teachers who are well educated and matured, in both the males and females. They are post graduate or above, hence their high qualification lends them towards radical attitudes.

It is found that in Lucknow University and its degree college teachers there is no significant difference between the attitude of male teachers from both levels.

It has been found that Lucknow University and its associated degree college teachers there is no significant difference between the attitudes of female teachers from both levels.

It has also been found that there is a significant difference between university male teachers and degree college female teachers, and there is not significant difference between Lucknow University male and female teachers' attitude.

It has also been found that there is a significant difference between degree college male and female teachers attitude.

When the present data was studied in accordance with three areas of life namely—personal, social and religious, it has been found that difference between male and female teachers are insignificant. It may be because the data are divided into three areas of life, which has resulted in making the differences as well as insignificant.

CONCLUSION

On the basis of above findings it is clear that most teachers are highly radical and radical in their personal, social and religious area of life and also they are modern but very few teachers (from the whole sample) are conservative (4.6%) and highly conservative (5.6) in their attitudes. Hence we can say that these agents of social change and communicator of knowledge are not involved in the conservatism.

On the basis of sex-wise analysis, it is clear that the male and female teachers of Lucknow University and its associated degree colleges have a different attitude towards radicalism and conservatism in three areas of life namely—personal, social and religious.

This means that one can accept the null hypothesis tested at 0.05 level of significance have a difference in university and degree college level, male and female teachers' attitude towards radicalism and conservatism.

The study also shows that there is a significant difference between male and female teachers of Lucknow University and its associated degree colleges male and male and between females and females.

The study also shows that there is no significant difference between male and female teachers' attitude in different areas of life namely—personal, social and religious area of life.

It is important to note that the above study was conducted within certain limitations. As stated earlier levels, (university and degree colleges), ranks (Professors, Readers, Lecturers) are not the only factors which has its influence on the attitude of university and degree colleges teachers (male and female). It is multidimensional and should be viewed from different angles and in different context. In each situation its influence may differ from one and another.

Chapter 10

Findings

Aforementioned description lays down a brief summary of the total work done. The descriptions below not only tells about ups and downs in the life of university and degree college teachers, but also society's reactions towards them, and the consequent changes brought in their life.

On the basis of thorough analysis of the present study summarized in the preceding paragraphs certain definite findings can be brought to light. Some of the major findings in this include, 59% teachers were male and 41% were female teachers from the university and college level, nearly three-fourths (68.7%) teachers were between the age group of 20-25 years. Maximum number of teachers represent Hindu community, (49.3%). It was entirely according to expectation as Hindus form the biggest stratum in Indian society. Similarly members of the upper caste Hindu who joined the teaching profession were 44.5% (Brahmin). The percentage of scheduled caste and backward was 7.4%. Muslims are holding the second position in population. The data regarding the Muslims shows that their percentage was 39%. Facts regarding the rank of university and college teachers that percentage of Readers and Lecturers and were high 41.6%.

Professors are less than Readers and Lecturers because Professors were available only at university level. Hence the percentage was 16.6%. Facts regarding family structure of the teachers tell that 81% teachers belong to nuclear families which is a modern trend. The joint families are being replaced by nuclear ones in society. In present study maximum number of teachers were married (66.6%). Regarding the income per month of teachers show that maximum number of teachers were in the middle income group (48.3%).

Therefore there was high percentage of Ph.D. holder teachers in the present study (83.3%). 10.33% teacher were D.Litt. holders while 7% were diploma holders and 11.7% teachers were gold medalist.

Facts regarding family composition of teachers tell that 36.3% teachers were eldest child of their parents. Parental make-up of university and associated degree colleges teachers house lays down that 45% teachers have lost their fathers but mothers were alive. Regarding educational status of university and associated degree colleges teachers' parents most of the fathers (41.6%) were highly educated and mothers (52.7%) were primary educated. These findings verifies the educational backwardness of women education in India. Investigation regarding the pattern of spending vacations of teachers shows that 73.3% teachers used to spend their vacations with family members. Hence it is true that the relationship of teachers with their family was harmonious. Data regarding the visit to family members shows that 50% teaches visit their relatives occasionally. Percentage of such teachers who make changes in the family was 69.3%. Regarding the adaptation of change in the family, analysis of the present study shows that 33.3% teachers' elders were oppose or resist the changes in the family 29.7% teachers younger resisted the change and 22.3% teachers elders and youngsters both opposed the changes only 14.7% teachers family members did not resisted the changes. Data regarding the tradition pattern in the family shows that 42.3% teachers have slightly changed pattern of tradition in their family. Almost all the teachers are from the nuclear families, hence the percentage of family members are not more than five to six. The percentage of one male was 64.6%. 51.7% were the single women of the family and 49.6% teachers had only one child in their families. Economy is a major factor to establish social and economic position of a person, data regarding the earning members in a family shows that 48.7% teachers had two earning members in the family, both husband and wife. Findings about the life partners' profession of university and college teachers shows that 31.7% teachers' life partners had teaching professions and 27.8% were not in teaching professions. 40.5% teachers life partners were house wives.

Data regarding the professional organizational setup of the respondents tell (77.3%) that there is not a political wing in their organizational setup. 100% teachers of the present study tell that they don't have any worship places in their educational institution and they do not fixed and amount in its maintenance. Today our country is facing many problems—national integration problem being one of them, as a agent of social change they discuss the current national problems, 90.7% teachers discuss national integration problems among the staff members. A maximum number of university and degree college teachers tell that caste and religion of difference is not working in educational institution, and they do not feel any caste feeling in their educational setup, the percentage of these teachers is 81 per cent.

Findings regarding the teachers activism shows that 15% teachers had participated in activism at school, college, university and professional levels. Data show that 9.3 per cent teachers had gone on hunger strike before and after joining the university. A maximum percentage (90.7%) of teachers had never gone on hunger strike. The investigation regarding the election contest 90.7% had never contested the election at any level, only 9.3% teachers had contested the election once, twice or more than two times. Data regarding the arrest record of police shows that most (85%) teachers had never been arrested by the police only 15% were arrested by the police before or after joining the university. Following facts have been found out regarding the socio-cultural activities of university and college teachers' behaviour. The data show that 65.7% teachers were attended the socio-cultural activities regularly. The detailed analysis of teachers' interest in politics shows that 88.4% teachers were interested in politics. The family background of teachers politics shows that 52.3% parents were not interested in the politics. A maximum number of teachers were not having any political leader in the family. Regarding for rejecting the political party, following findings have been brought to life. 28% teachers of university and degree colleges tell that they don't have any specific reason for rejecting the political party and 26% teachers had rejected the political party due to their teaching profession. Findings regarding the interest level of politics shows that 51% teachers were interested in their national politics. Teachers said that the 95.3% did not like communalism and communal riots. They opined that religious persons are responsible for communal tensions (53.3%). 78.3% teachers told that the recent major problem of Mandir-Masjid issue was not in favour of the country, 78.3% teachers had said it. Investigation revealed that most teachers (68.4%) wished that government should take the decision to solve the Mandir-Masjid issue. On the major problem of the country 41.7% teachers said that unemployment is the biggest problem. Government should try to solve these problems. 56% teachers were satisfied with the efforts done by the government. Investigations regarding the ideological orientation of university and college teachers shows that 83.3% teachers were ideologically oriented, in which 48.3% teachers were rightists and 35% were leftist ideologically oriented.

Following facts have been found out regarding attitudes of the university and its associated degree college teachers with respect to their sex, age, qualification in three areas of life namely—personal, social and religious. The findings shows that most teachers were highly radical (36.6%) and only 5.6% were highly conservative. Data regarding the male and female teachers of university and degree colleges shows that there is no significant difference between male and female teachers. The analysis of university and degree college male teachers shows that there is not a significant difference between university and degree college male teachers attitude. In case of female teachers from both levels, the difference between two mean was 0.17 which was not significant at 0.05 and 0.01 level. The present attitude analysis shows that university male teachers and degree college female teachers attitude (2) were significant at 0.05 level. Hence Ho was rejected at 0.05 level of significance. Data regarding the male and female teachers of Lucknow University shows that the difference between two mean was 53 which was not significant at either level (0.05 and 0.01). The difference of two mean between degree college male and female teachers were 3.7, which was highly significant at both levels, hence the investigator had rejected the null hypothesis at 0.05 level and 0.01 level. To find out the relationship between age and attitude the investigator classifies the teachers into two groups, above 40 years and 40 and below 40 years. Both mean differences were not significant at either level. Hence Ho was retained at 0.05 and 0.01 level significance. Investigation regarding the qualification of teachers, the sample was categorized into two groups above post graduate and only post graduate, finding shows that difference was not significant at either level. Data regarding the personal area of university and degree college teachers on the basis of their sex shows that the obtained difference was 73 which was not significant at 0.05 level. To analyze the attitude of male and female teachers in social area of life, the data was categorized into two groups, the obtained difference was 95, which was not significant at either level. The attitude of male and female teachers of university and degree colleges in religious area of life shows that the obtained difference was 41 which was not significant at their level.

Chapter 11
Conclusion

People differ in their behaviour towards conservatism and radicalism. One person may greet every change with joy considering it a step towards a better society. There are other type of people who dread changes, they look back to the good old days. These differences in attitude and behaviour tend to fall somewhere along a conservative, radical continuum, some where between opposing and favouring social change.

Change is an essential feature of society. Man as an organism is a good example of change. Through a process of socialization man from his birth to old age passes through many stages. The economist take change in terms of wants and needs but the sociologist and as Durkheim, describe this change in terms of relationship and interdependence. In this regard teachers play a vital role in shaping new pattern of relationship and interdependence of society. The university and college teachers are more important than the other teachers, because their students are generally more attached to them emotionally as well as psychologically. The attitudes of the students is influenced by many factors and the personality and behaviour of a teacher is one of them. This is the reason that the teacher should be open minded, progressive and radical so that the student should be positively influenced towards radicalism.

Education, both formal and informal as life experience, is a social institution sharing in society and participating in the transactional process. Radical ideas, in society in other social institution, and in regard to education itself have the potential of great or modest change in the way of think about students, teachers, curriculum and learning. Mass free public education was a radical idea of the earlier times. After passing of the time, the educational institutions are even more conservative in their patterns of change than the general society because they are perceived as the protectors of the past. Teachers are still being fired or reassigned for raising questions about the norms and values of the society. No one in recent times has met the fate of Socrates, who challenged the popular ideas of his time and was condemned to die for corrupting the morals of youth, but many have felt a similar wrath from the society. As an educator he raised serious questions about man and society. This radical education was met by a radical response, and Socrates' resulting death. Life and education are closely associated, one having its inevitable impact on the other. Since the World War II there have been revolutionary changes in the various walks of life all over the world. After the achievement of political independence in 1947, we became engaged in re-planning our educational system in consonance with the emerging democracy in the land. Education Commission (1966) expressed "of all the different factors which influence the quality of education and its contribution to the national development, the quality, competence and character of teachers are undoubtedly the most significant."

The emphasis of the present study has all along been on deep analysis of the observed data. It is hoped that extensive review of the literature found in each of the preceding chapters will be of some help to future research scholars interested in this field. Guided by the existing body of knowledge in each topic the findings of the present study have been analyzed and discussed in considerable detail. Starting with a straight description of the findings data in each topic has been tabulated against a number of relevant variables. The attitude of university and degree college teachers have been analyzed with respect to their age, sex and qualification. This mode of the quantitative analysis is fairly common in the field of psychology whereas in sociology emphasis so far has been mostly on descriptive and interesting analysis of the observed findings.

The attitudes of the students are influenced by many factors, teachers and their attitudes are one of them. This is the reason that a college and university teachers' should be open minded, progressive and radical, so that the students should be positively influenced towards radicalism. Teachers behaviour influences the behaviour of the students', hence a conservative teacher would influence hundreds of students and the result would be that hundreds of conservatives would be there to hinder the progress of nation, whereas a radical teacher would influence hundreds of students towards progressive ideas and radicalism. Hence it is more important that radical teacher should be more.

This is being mostly suggested that in spite of socio-economic differences in the background of teachers, similar and good performance during the teaching should be assured. As every teacher has to work to get somewhere, his knowledge of the teaching will decide the fate of educational institution and organization.

A conservative teacher always plays with the teaching profession and students mind. Since every student and every institution is equally significant, therefore the teachers must teach with complete knowledge. University and college teachers produced two kinds of impacts with their teaching acts. First the proper working of the teaching is assured and secondly their own teaching skill is tested. Therefore, teaching is rightfully well equipped with practical knowledge, in spite of the different teaching methods. It is observed that most teachers are radical in their personal, social and religious areas of life, so teachers those who a architect of a new generation are not involve in conservatism they are radical only in spite of few teachers. It is sad that these few teachers and the result would be that hundreds of conservatives would be there to hinder the progress of the nation. It is necessary for the democratic secular India that there should be more and more radical teachers in our colleges and university.

Following were the limitations of the present study. The study has covered only a few colleges located in Lucknow city. The study is confined to the University of Lucknow and its associated degree colleges only, the study include teachers belonging to the graduate and post graduate level. The present study has covered only University and few degree colleges of the Lucknow city. Related to it, several other investigations can be done. The same study, can be conducted on university level teachers belonging to different castes, community and faculties. A research project can be undertaken to study the attitudes of teachers towards radicalism and conservation in various types of colleges such as Engineering colleges, arts college, medical colleges and the religious institutions. A study like this can be conducted on school teachers and college teachers behaviour towards conservatism and radicalism.

The main aim of the present study has been confined only to assess the Lucknow University and its affiliated degree college teachers' behaviour at the scale of conservatism and radicalism. The purpose of the study was to find out a difference between male and female teachers' behaviour regarding their conservatism and radicalism elements in personal, social and religious area of life. To assess the attitude of male and female teachers of Lucknow University and degree college teachers a five point scale had been applied by the investigator. The results shows that almost teachers from both levels (University and degree college) were highly radical, but only few teachers in the present educational institutions were conservative. It has become necessary for the national integrity that they should be open minded and radical at a time; because our pupils are the future of our country if they are conservative the whole country would be suffered from this disease like, communalism, regionalism, linguism, terrorism and casteism etc. At present the Mandir-Masjid issue has assumed bigger shape, it is now total national issue. Mandir-Masjid issue is a part of communalism and conservatism. Conservatism is provoked on the basis of certain man-made issue. That issue is propagated on large scale, conservative feelings are exploited to a great extent. Then with one appropriate stroke rioting is made to burst and it wraps the entire society.

Teachers in the true sense of the term is a transforming personality. Rightly it has been remarked that the teacher is not an instructor or a task master but also a helper and a guide. Thus the university and college teachers should be radical, progressive, open minded at a time. The university and college teachers should be quoted as, "The nation builder, torch bearer, maker of man and agent of social change towards a radical society."

Bibliography

Anderson, G.E. *Three Worlds of Capitalism*, Polity Press, Cambridge, 1990.

Appadurai, A. *Indian Political Thinking Through the Ages*, Khanna Publisher's, New Delhi, 1992.

Appadurai, A., *Modernity at Large Cultural Dimensions of Globalization*, New Delhi. Oxford University Press, 1997.

Aloysius, G. *Nationalism without a Nation in India*, N. Delhi, Oxford University, 1997.

Arnason, J.P. *History of Civilizational Analysis*, In Encyclopedia of the Social and Behavioural Sciences. London Elsevier, 2001.

Aggarwal, Y.P. Higher Education in the context of Planned Development, in Power, K.B. and Panda, S.K. (eds.), *Higher Education In India—In Search of Quality*, N. Delhi AIU, 1995.

AIU Universities Handbook, New Delhi, AIU 1997

Altbach, P.G. *The Dilemma of Change in Indian Higher Education*, Higher Education, 1993.

2002 Antinomies of Society: *Essays on Ideologies and Institutions*. N.Delhi. Oxford University Press.

Arnason, J.P. *Civilization in Dispute*, London: Sage.

A.B. Wolf, *Conservatism, Radicalism and Scientific Method*.

A Hand book of Sociology, Preface by Karl Manhhem, Ogbam William F and Mimkoff Meyer.

A Hand book of Sociology by Raka Saran.

Babri Masjid-Ram Janam Bhoomi Controversy N. Delhi: Ajanta Publications, 1990.

British Journal of Sociology Vol. XIII, (1962)

Crittenden, J. *Beyond Individualism Reconstituting the Liberal Self*. Oxford: Oxford University Press 1992.

Clinton Rossiter, *Conservatism in America: The Thankless Persuation*, Second Edition, New York: vintage Bookd, 1962

College Teachers-Challenges and Responses, by Arun. P. Bali

College Teachers. Their Problems and Solutions. Educational Review 73, Atma Ram, 7th July (1967). 71. Bibliography on Higher Education in India, New Frontiers of Education, (1975).

Conservatism - Radicalism measured by immediate emotional reactions, *Journal of Social Psychology*, Alport R. and Sargent S.S. IXV (1941).

Conservatism - Radicalism measured by immediate emotional reactions, *Journal of Social Psychology*. IXV (1941)

Conservatism Radicalism in international *Encyclopedia of the Social Sciences*, ed. D.L. Sills, New Yark, XII (1968).

Conservatism the only way, Reginald Northam.

Conservative Man, Bottomore Tom. *The New York Review of Books*, Vol XV (1970).

Critique of Profession as a Sociological Category, Robert Habenstain, *Sociological Quarterly* 4, (1963).

"Dhar Punnalal, India and Her domestic problems", *Religion, State and Secularism*, Calcutta, Punthi Pustak, 1993.

Dutt R.C. (ed.) *People and Politics: The Indian Experience*, N. Delhi, Lancer Publishers, 1992

Derrett, J.D.M., *Religion, Law and the State in India,* Oxford University Press, 1999.

Dube, Leela, *Women and Kinship: Comparative Perspectives on Gender in South-East Asia,* Tokyo: The United Nations University, 1997.

Dhawa Rajeev, *Constitutional Rhetoric and Right to Education Indian Express,* N. Delhi, August 10, 1992.

D'sanzer, P.R. Democracy and National Integration: Political rationalities in Ali Ashraf (ed.) *Ethinic Identity and National Integration* N. Delhi, Concept, 1994.

Dictionary of Sociology by Fairchild H.P. London, Vision Press.

Engineer, Asghar Ali (Ed.), *Mandal Commission Controversy,* Ajanta Publications, Delhi, 1991.

Eder, C, Does Social Class Matter in the study of Social Movements: A Theory of Middle-Class Radicalism, in L. Maheu (Ed.) *Social Movements and Social Classes:* The Future of Collective Action, London, Sage.

Early Changes in teacher attitude, Jet Journal of Education for Teaching, Hogben O. and Petty M.F. (1979).

Education in Changing India by, K.L. Shrimali

Education in India Today and Tomorrow, Baroda, Acharya Book depot. (1957).

Essays on Sociology and Social Psychology, Karl Mannheim 38. A Philosophy for a Modern Man, H. Levy.

Foley M. (Ed.) *Ideas that Shape Politics,* Manchestar University Press, Manchester, 1994.

From School to University - A Study with Special Reference to University, Engerence (1954).

Hasan, M.K. and Sarkar, S.N., Attitude towards caste system as related to certain personality and sociological factors' *Indian Journal of Psychology,* 1975.

Hastings, A: *The Construction of Nationhood: Ethnicity, Religion and Nationalism*, Cambridge: Cambridge University Press.

Human Problems in Technological Change by Spicer.

Inkeles A, The modernization of man is weiher; M (ed.) Modernization: The Dynamics of Growth, VALE, 1996.

Ideology and the Development of Sociological Therory, Zeitlin I.M., New Jersey (1968).

Ideology and Utopia, An Introducing to the Sociology of Knowledge, Karl Mannheim.

Islam and the Integration of Society, W. Montgomery Walt.

Kakkar, Sudhir, *The Colours of Violence*, N. Delhi, Penguin Books, 1995.

Kashyap, Subhash (ed.) *National Policy Studies*, Tata McGraw-Hill, N. Delhi, 1990.

Knowledge, Education and Cultural Change, Richard Brown.

Lorenzi-ciold, F Self-Stereo-typing and self-enhancement in gender groups. *European Journal of Personality and Social Psychology*, 1991.

Mazzin, Ali M., The need for special rights for minorities: Some international and Indian Dimensions, *Journal of Objective Studies*, N. Delhi, 1992.

Madan, T.N. *Myths and Locked Minds: Secularism and Fundamentalism in India*, Oxford University Press, N.,Delhi 1997.

Ministry of Human Resource Development, *Programme of Action*, N. Delhi, MHRD, 1992.

Mukhopadhyay, M., 'Globalization Imperatives for Indian Education Sector', *University New-35*, May 18, 1997.

Martin Shaw, "The coming crises of Radical Sociology", in Robin Blackburn (Ed.), op. cit. p. 43.

Measured of radicalism - conservatism, *Journal of Social Psychology*, L XVIII (1965).

Modernization and Social Change by Rajendra Pandey.

Nandy Ashis, Shikha Trivedi Shail Mayaram Achyat Yagnik, *Creating a Nationality Delhi*: Oxford University Press, 1995.

NLM, *Evaluation of Literacy Compaigns in India*: Report of the Exports Group, N. Delhi. Directorate of Adult Education, 1994.

Prosser, M & Trigwell, K. Relations between Perceptions of the Teaching Environment and Approaches to Teaching. *British Journal of Educational Psychology*, 1997.

Prosser M & Trigwell, K. Understanding learning and teaching: The experience in higher education, Buckingham, U. K: The Society for Research into Higher Education and Open University Press.

Personality Difference among Conservative and Progressive Ladies Research, *Journal of Philosophy and Social Sciences*, II (1965).

Personality Differences among Conservative and Progressive Ladies, *Research Journal of Philosophy and Social Sciences*, II (1965).

Personality Traits related to Conservatism and Radicalism, *Journal of Character Personality*, VII (1939).

Polish Peasant in Europe and America, W.I. Thomas and Znaniecki, (1958).

Progress, *Journal of Ethics*, Human Nature and conduct, Bewy J. New York, (1922).

Rao, K. Raghavendra, *Religion, Society and State*, N. Delhi, ICSSR, Publications, 1992.

Radical Ideas and the Schools, Edited by Jack. L. Neison, Kenneth Carison, Thomas. E. Linton Holt, Rinehart and Winston, Inc. New York. 1972.

Radical Man, The Process of Psycho-social Development, by Charles Hampden-Turner (1969).

Radical Paradoxes, Dilemmas of the America Left - 1940-1970 edited by Peter Clescak, Harper and Row Publishers, New York, Evanston.

Radical Prospective on Social Problems, by Frame Linderfild. The Mac Millian Company, New York, (1961).

Radical Sociology Edited by J. David Colfax and Jack. L. Roach, New York (1971).

Radical Sociology, An Introduction by David Horowitz, Canfield Press, San Francisco (1971).

Radicalism Conservatism and Scientific Method, Wholfe A.B., New York (1923).

Raicalism in a Dictionary of Social Sciences ed. Julius Gould and Wil Kolb, New York, Free Press (1964).

Repot - New Delhi, Ministry of Education, India Education Commission (1966).

Research in Education, Best J.W. Prentice, New Delhi. (1982).

Srinivas, M.N. *On Living in a Revolution and Other Essays*, Delhi: Oxford University Press, 1992.

Sharma, G.D., Staff Development programmes in Higher Education, in Power, K.B. and S.K. Panda, (eds.) *Higher Education in India: In Search of Quality*, N. Delhi, AIU, 1995.

She Who Rises a Peacock, Cormack, Bombay, Asia Publishing House, (1961).

Social Change, An Analysis of Attitudes and Personality, Vasudeva P. New Delhi (1976).

Social Change by Walterstain.

Social Problems in our Time by Krinson Weinherg, Roosevelt University (1960).

Social Purpose of Education, K.G. Cpllier.

Social Structure and Personality by Talcot Parsons.

Social Theory and Social Structure, Merten, R.K. New York, (1968).

Sociologist and Social Change in India Today, Mukherji, Ramkrishan.

Sociology and Behaviour, Barash D.P.

Sociology and Education and School, Burgess.

Sociology and the Sterotype of the Criminal, by Chapman, oennis.

Sociology of Teaching, Willard Walter.

Sociology of the Profession by Elliott.

Sociology of the teaching Profession in India, Ruhela Satya Pal.

Statistical Methods, Gupta S.P. New Delhi, (1977).

Stutistics in Psychology and Education, Garrett H.E. (1966).

Takwale, R.G. Indira Gandhi National Open University in the Twenty First Century in, Power, K.B. and Panda (Eds.) *Higher Education in India-In Search of Quality,* N. Delhi: AIU, 1995.

Tawney, R.H. *The Radical Tradition,* London, George, Allen & Un-in, 1964.

T.B. Bottomore, *Entities of Society: Radical Though in North America,* New York: Pantheon Book, 1968.

Teachers as a Professional Group and their organizations, Aurora, G.S., NCERT, New Delhi (1970).

Techniques of Teaching, Peterson A.D.C. Oxford (1965).

The Coming Crisis of Western Sociology, Gouldner A.W., London (1970).

The End of Ideology, Beli Daniel, New York, (1960).

The Fundamental Forms of Social Thought by Stark Werner, (1962).

The Sociology of Welfare, Graham Room.

The Three Spheres of Society, Charles Waterman.

The Universities, Green, V.H.H., Penguin Books, (1969).

Tom Bottomore, "conservative man". *The New York Review of Books*. October, 1970.

Towards a general theory of action - Talcott Parsons and Edward A. Shils, Harvard University Press Cambridge, Masachusetts, (1954).

Towards the Sociology of Knowledge, Remling W.

Young People and Society, by Tapper, Tend.

Index

❑❑❑